Dil Chahta Hai Soundtrack

33 1/3 Global

33 1/3 Global, a series related to but independent from **33 1/3**, takes the format of the original series of short, music-based books and brings the focus to music throughout the world. With initial volumes focusing on Japanese and Brazilian music, the series will also include volumes on the popular music of Australia/Oceania, Europe, Africa, the Middle East, and more.

33 1/3 Japan

Series Editor: Noriko Manabe

Spanning a range of artists and genres—from the 1970s rock of Happy End to technopop band Yellow Magic Orchestra, the Shibuya-kei of Cornelius, classic anime series *Cowboy Bebop*, J-Pop/EDM hybrid Perfume, and vocaloid star Hatsune Miku—33 1/3 Japan is a series devoted to in-depth examination of Japanese popular music of the twentieth and twenty-first centuries.

Published Titles:
Supercell's *Supercell* by Keisuke Yamada
AKB48 by Patrick W. Galbraith and Jason G. Karlin
Yoko Kanno's *Cowboy Bebop Soundtrack* by Rose Bridges
Perfume's *Game* by Patrick St. Michel
Cornelius's *Fantasma* by Martin Roberts
Joe Hisaishi's *My Neighbor Totoro: Soundtrack* by Kunio Hara
Shonen Knife's *Happy Hour* by Brooke McCorkle
Nenes' *Koza Dabasa* by Henry Johnson
Yuming's *The 14th Moon* by Lasse Lehtonen
Toshiko Akiyoshi-Lew Tabackin Big Band's *Kogun* by E. Taylor Atkins

Forthcoming Titles:
Yellow Magic Orchestra's *Yellow Magic Orchestra* by Toshiyuki Ohwada
Kohaku utagassen's *The Red and White Song Contest* by Shelley Brunt
S.O.B.'s *Don't Be Swindle* by Mahon Murphy and Ran Zwigenberg

33 1/3 Brazil

Series Editor: Jason Stanyek

Covering the genres of samba, tropicália, rock, hip hop, forró, bossa nova, heavy metal and funk, among others, 33 1/3 Brazil is a series devoted to in-depth examination of the most important Brazilian albums of the twentieth and twenty-first centuries.

Published Titles:
Caetano Veloso's *A Foreign Sound* by Barbara Browning
Tim Maia's *Tim Maia Racional Vols. 1 & 2* by Allen Thayer
João Gilberto and Stan Getz's *Getz/Gilberto* by Brian McCann
Gilberto Gil's *Refazenda* by Marc A. Hertzman
Dona Ivone Lara's *Sorriso Negro* by Mila Burns
Milton Nascimento and Lô Borges's *The Corner Club* by Jonathon Grasse
Racionais MCs' *Sobrevivendo no Inferno* by Derek Pardue
Naná Vasconcelos's *Saudades* by Daniel B. Sharp
Chico Buarque's First *Chico Buarque* by Charles A. Perrone

Forthcoming titles:
Jorge Ben Jor's *África Brasil* by Frederick J. Moehn

33 1/3 Europe

Series Editor: Fabian Holt

Spanning a range of artists and genres, 33 1/3 Europe offers engaging accounts of popular and culturally significant albums of Continental Europe and the North Atlantic from the twentieth and twenty-first centuries.

Published Titles:
Darkthrone's *A Blaze in the Northern Sky* by Ross Hagen
Ivo Papazov's *Balkanology* by Carol Silverman
Heiner Müller and Heiner Goebbels's *Wolokolamsker Chaussee* by Philip V. Bohlman
Modeselektor's *Happy Birthday!* by Sean Nye

Mercyful Fate's *Don't Break the Oath* by Henrik Marstal
Bea Playa's *I'll Be Your Plaything* by Anna Szemere and András Rónai
Various Artists' *DJs do Guetto* by Richard Elliott
Czesław Niemen's *Niemen Enigmatic* by Ewa Mazierska and Mariusz Gradowski
Massada's *Astaganaga* by Lutgard Mutsaers
Los Rodriguez's *Sin Documentos* by Fernán del Val and Héctor Fouce
Édith Piaf's *Récital 1961* by David Looseley
Nuovo Canzoniere Italiano's *Bella Ciao* by Jacopo Tomatis
Iannis Xenakis's *Persepolis* by Aram Yardumian
Vopli Vidopliassova's *Tantsi* by Maria Sonevytsky
Amália Rodrigues's *Amália at the Olympia* by Lila Ellen Gray
Ardit Gjebrea's *Projekt Jon* by Nicholas Tochka
Aqua's *Aquarium* by C.C. McKee
Einstürzende Neubauten's *Kollaps* by Melle Jan Kromhout and Jan Nieuwenhuis
J.M.K.E.'s *To the Cold Land* by Brigitta Davidjants

Forthcoming Titles:
Taco Hemingway's *Jarmark* by Kamila Rymajdo
Tripes' *Kefali Gemato Hrisafi* by Dafni Tragaki
Silly's *Februar* by Michael Rauhut
CCCP's *Fedeli Alla Linea's 1964–1985 Affinità-Divergenze Fra Il Compagno Togliatti E Noi Del Conseguimento Della Maggiore Età* by Giacomo Bottà
Sigur Rós' *Ágætis Byrjun* by Tore Størvold

33 1/3 Oceania

Series Editors: Jon Stratton (senior editor) and Jon Dale (specializing in books on albums from Aotearoa/New Zealand)

Spanning a range of artists and genres from Australian Indigenous artists to Maori and Pasifika artists, from Aotearoa/New Zealand noise music to Australian rock, and including music from Papua and other Pacific islands, 33 1/3 Oceania offers exciting accounts of albums that illustrate the wide range of music made in the Oceania region.

Published Titles:
John Farnham's *Whispering Jack* by Graeme Turner
The Church's *Starfish* by Chris Gibson
Regurgitator's *Unit* by Lachlan Goold and Lauren Istvandity
Kylie Minogue's *Kylie* by Adrian Renzo and Liz Giuffre
Alastair Riddell's *Space Waltz* by Ian Chapman
Hunters & Collectors's *Human Frailty* by Jon Stratton
The Front Lawn's *Songs from the Front Lawn* by Matthew Bannister
Bic Runga's *Drive* by Henry Johnson
The Dead C's *Clyma est mort* by Darren Jorgensen
Ed Kuepper's *Honey Steel's Gold* by John Encarnacao
Chain's *Toward the Blues* by Peter Beilharz
Hilltop Hoods' *The Calling* by Dianne Rodger
Screamfeeder's *Kitten Licks* by Ben Green and Ian Rogers
Soundtrack from *Saturday Night Fever* by Clinton Walker

Forthcoming Titles:
The Triffids' *Born Sandy Devotional* by Christina Ballico
Crowded House's *Together Alone* by Barnaby Smith
5MMM's *Compilation Album of Adelaide Bands 1980* by Collette Snowden
The Clean's *Boodle Boodle Boodle* by Geoff Stahl
INXS' *Kick* by Ryan Daniel and Lauren Moxey
Sunnyboys' *Sunnyboys* by Stephen Bruel
Eyeliner's *Buy Now* by Michael Brown
Silverchair's *Frogstomp* by Jay Daniel Thompson
TISM's *Machiavelli and the Four Seasons* by Tyler Jenke
The La De Das' *The Happy Prince* by John Tebbutt
John Sangster's *Lord of the Rings, Vols. 1–3* by Bruce Johnson
Gary Shearston's *Dingo* by Peter Mills
The Avalanches' *Since I Left You* by Charles Fairchild
Kate Ceberano's *Brave* by Panizza Allmark
Robert Forster's *Danger in the Past* by Patrick Chapman
Various Artists' *A Truckload of Sky: The Lost Songs of David McComb* by Glenn D'Cruz

33 1/3 South Asia

Series Editor: Natalie Sarrazin

From the films of Bollywood and Lollywood, to home-grown *bhangra* hip-hop, Hindu devotional pop and Sufi rock, Sri Lankan rap, Indo jazz and disco, new-wave electronica and diasporic Asian Underground scene, 33 1/3 South Asia takes readers on a sonically diverse journey through the most significant soundtracks and albums from the twentieth and twenty-first centuries.

Published:
Dil Chahta Hai Soundtrack by Jayson Beaster-Jones

Forthcoming:
Coke Studio (Season 14) by Rakae Rehman Jamil and Khadija Muzaffar
Lata Mangeshkar's *My Favourites, Volume 2* by Anirudha Bhattacharjee and Chandrashekhar Rao

Dil Chahta Hai Soundtrack

Jayson Beaster-Jones

Series Editor: Natalie Sarrazin

BLOOMSBURY ACADEMIC
NEW YORK • LONDON • OXFORD • NEW DELHI • SYDNEY

BLOOMSBURY ACADEMIC
Bloomsbury Publishing Inc
1385 Broadway, New York, NY 10018, USA
50 Bedford Square, London, WC1B 3DP, UK
29 Earlsfort Terrace, Dublin 2, Ireland

BLOOMSBURY, BLOOMSBURY ACADEMIC and the Diana logo
are trademarks of Bloomsbury Publishing Plc

First published in the United States of America 2024

Copyright © Jayson Beaster-Jones, 2024

For legal purposes the Acknowledgments on pp. xx–xxi constitute an
extension of this copyright page.

All rights reserved. No part of this publication may be reproduced
or transmitted in any form or by any means, electronic or
mechanical, including photocopying, recording, or any
information storage or retrieval system, without prior
permission in writing from the publishers.

Bloomsbury Publishing Inc does not have any control over, or responsibility
for, any third-party websites referred to or in this book. All internet addresses
given in this book were correct at the time of going to press. The author and
publisher regret any inconvenience caused if addresses have changed or sites
have ceased to exist, but can accept no responsibility for any such changes.

Whilst every effort has been made to locate copyright holders
the publishers would be grateful to hear from any person(s)
not here acknowledged.

Library of Congress Cataloging-in-Publication Data
Names: Beaster-Jones, Jayson, author.
Title: Dil Chahta Hai soundtrack / Jayson Beaster-Jones.
Description: [1.] | New York : Bloomsbury Academic, 2024. |
Series: 33 1/3 South Asia | Includes bibliographical references and index.
Identifiers: LCCN 2024019906 (print) | LCCN 2024019907 (ebook) |
ISBN 9781501388668 (paperback) | ISBN 9781501388651 (hardback) |
ISBN 9781501388675 (ebook) | ISBN 9781501388682 (pdf)
Subjects: LCSH: Shankar Ehsaan Loy (Musical group). Dil Chahta Hai. |
Dil Chahta Hai (Motion picture) | Motion picture music–India–History and
criticism. | Film soundtracks–India–History and criticism. | Motion picture
industry–India–Mumbai. | Film composers–India–Interviews.
Classification: LCC ML2075 .B39 2024 (print) | LCC ML2075 (ebook) |
DDC 781.5/420954–dc23/eng/20240502
LC record available at https://lccn.loc.gov/2024019906
LC ebook record available at https://lccn.loc.gov/2024019907

ISBN:	HB:	978-1-5013-8865-1
	PB:	978-1-5013-8866-8
	ePDF:	978-1-5013-8868-2
	eBook:	978-1-5013-8867-5

Typeset by Integra Software Services Pvt. Ltd.

Series: 33 1/3 South Asia

To find out more about our authors and books visit www.bloomsbury.com and
sign up for our newsletters.

Contents

Preface x
Note about Translation and Transliteration xviii
Acknowledgments xx

Part I **The Soundtrack** 1

1   *Dil Chahta Hai* **Contexts** 3

2   **Shankar-Ehsaan-Loy's Rock Band Aesthetic** 19

3   **The Rock Band Aesthetic in** *Dil Chahta Hai* 29

4   *Dil Chahta Hai*'s **Reception and Influence** 49

Part II **Interviews** 55

5   **Interview—Ehsaan Noorani (Composer, Musician)** 57

6   **Interview—Loy Mendonsa (Composer, Musician)** 77

7   **Interview—Vijay Benegal (Lead Recording and Mixing Engineer)** 95

8   **Interview—Michael Harvey (Composer)** 113

Personnel 118
Works Cited 119
Index 125

Preface

It is 2021, twenty years after the release of Shankar-Ehsaan-Loy's landmark soundtrack *Dil Chahta Hai*. I am listening closely to the entire album again for the first time in perhaps ten years. This time I am wearing noise-canceling headphones, and the sound envelops me in much the same way I might have experienced by watching the film in the theater (although in the case of *Dil Chahta Hai*, my first viewing took place by way of a pirated DVD purchased at a store in north Chicago—I had purchased the CD of the soundtrack in a 2002 trip to Mumbai). In this listen, the recording is crisp, the instruments placed in space around me. The bass has depth and generates a solid groove that brings me along, cajoling my body to move along to the beat. Ehsaan Noorani's searing rock guitar riffs and solos are unlike anything I had heard in Bollywood up to that point. Now, I am hearing them for the first time again and realizing this fact: this soundtrack hasn't aged one bit.

Although I am listening closely to the soundtrack for the first time in a while, I have taught *Dil Chahta Hai* (hereafter *DCH*) many times in my Bollywood film classes over the last twenty years. Each time I teach the film, I indicate to my students that *DCH* marks a transition in Hindi cinema in the twenty-first century. The buddy film in Bollywood is not a new innovation, of course—there are plenty of examples over the last fifty years. Rather, *DCH* marks an aesthetic departure for Indian cinema, as it unapologetically portrays youthful, urban, upper-middle class life in Mumbai, *à la* the hit American TV show *Friends* (a show which, incidentally, many of my Indian friends watched religiously on satellite television in the early 2000s). The film presents an Indian youth that travels overseas, that is comfortable being Indian abroad, has tastes in international music, that lives an enviable lifestyle. This "naturalistic" representation of India's casually wealthy class was a point of both positive and negative reviews of the film. Unlike most films of the 1980s and 1990s, overseas travel for young Indian men and women does not provoke an identity crisis, it is just something that people do. It's a comfortable space. It captures the idealized sense of "globalization" that social theorists like Arjun Appadurai (1996) were discussing at the end of the 1990s: the sometimes seamless movement of people, finance capital, media, and ideas across national borders. In so many ways, *DCH* represents the early optimism of globalization as it portrayed the fruits of new social and political systems ushered in by India's economic reforms of the 1990s. These social and economic transformations have often been represented as a political U-turn from Gandhian austerity politics. The film is saturated with this optimism, this youthful effervescence, as the Akash, Sid, and Sameer travel first to the former Portuguese colony of Goa (which has long been a reliable "other" for Indian cinema), then go their separate ways, only to come back together again.

While the narrative of *DCH* centers around a trio of friends, the music of DCH centers upon the music director trio Shankar-Ehsaan-Loy. SEL, as their fans call them, similarly present the voice of exuberance and in doing so, make *DCH* one of the defining soundtracks of the first decade of the twenty-first century. If at its height in the 1960s and 1970s rock music in the United States and UK represented a moment of youthful, collective energy stemming from rebellion against social norms of deprivation, SEL's soundtrack to *DCH* captures a similar kind of energy at a similar inflection point in Indian history. On this basis, one might further say that *Dil Chahta Hai* hits its mark as one of the watershed soundtracks in the history of Indian cinema. The irony is, of course, that none of the boys portrayed in the film seems to have experienced deprivations of their parents and grandparents. But that's the film world for you.

Beyond these broader themes of globalization, I focus my students' attention on the duets "Woh Ladki Hai Kahan" (Where is that girl?) and "Jaane Kyon Log Pyar Karte Hai" (Who knows why people fall in love?) when I teach the film. Both of these songs prominently feature instruments and sounds from outside of India: Irish tin whistle and fiddle in the former, Australian didgeridoo in the latter. These songs have a vibrancy to them that buoys the film and the soundtrack. The picturization (the colloquial term for the cinematography) of these songs is similarly playful. "Woh Ladki" is set in a posh Mumbai movie theater. The song presents the characters in a music video—they are simultaneously sitting in the theater and watching their relationship blossom as a timeless romance across the decades. The cinematography riffs off the visual style of film directors Raj Kapoor, Dev Anand, and others, setting the hero and heroine of the sequence in the context of great Indian love stories, but in a thoroughly contemporary way. This trope of representing a simulated past in terms of the present through the use of digital camera filters became a technique used by many later cinematographers of the early twenty-first century. The music is joyous, as are the voices of the hero and heroine (the Indipop singer Shaan and playback singer Kavita Krishnamurthy) as their voices intertwine and develop the love story of the film. Underlying the track is the "Bo Diddley" guitar riff (i.e., a modified *son clave*) that holds the song together rhythmically, while Irish tin whistle and fiddle provide a bouncy accompaniment. As I will point out later, "Woh Ladki" melds the verse-chorus form of international rock music with the typical *mukhda-antara* lyrical form of Hindi film songs. This is one of the songs supporting my claim that *DCH* foundationally develops a rock band aesthetic for Hindi cinema.

The other duet, "Jaane Kyon," is set in Sydney, Australia. It similarly develops a romantic visual narrative, as the characters take in the local sites while accompanied by music that portrays the Australian experience. Singer Udit Narayan's flirtatious, teasing vocal delivery contrasts with the earnestness of singer Alka Yagnik, creating a delicious friction between two perspectives on romantic love. Beyond the exotic sounds and the vocal renditions, this is a music video that could have just as easily been filmed by the Australian Tourism Board as by the award winning cinematographer Ravi K. Chandran. I've written about these songs and their musical aesthetic elsewhere, but there is a lot more to say. I will cover much more detail in later chapters of this book.

DCH is not SEL's first soundtrack, nor is it their most popular or their best (to my mind). But it is one of their most important, as it presents a new trajectory for Indian film songs in the twenty-first century. As I will suggest, SEL provided an alternative sound to A. R. Rahman's "New Bollywood" (Booth 2008) orientation. Also like Rahman, and every other music director in Hindi language cinema before him, the trio is attuned to international sounds and styles and stirs these influences liberally into their compositions and performances. In my other academic publications (Beaster-Jones 2015), I refer to this practice of fusing sounds from different musical traditions as "mediation," as the people who compose and produce music are very intentional about the kinds of sounds and styles that they synthesize into their songs. They are quite cognizant of the fact that these sounds and styles need to be transformed—that is, mediated—in order to be made palatable to the audiences that they hope to attract. The bigger point that I will be making throughout this book is that *DCH* provided an additional template for mediation of local and international styles that enabled both the success of many subsequent music directors, and the rapid transformation of the sounds and the structures of Indian popular music in the first decades of the twenty-first century.

Dil Chahta Hai and *33 1/3*

In reading through the series, I have noticed that other books in the *33 1/3* catalog have taken circuitous routes in addressing the albums that they discuss. Most of the authors presume a deep knowledge and fanbase for the albums that they are discussing, which is probably pretty accurate in the broader context of the American and British music industries. I anticipate that the intended audiences for those books are people already familiar with historical contexts out of which those albums emerge and the conventions these albums deploy and transform. These books can thus effectively reference and draw attention to large bodies of shared cultural and historical knowledge to contextualize these albums with minimum signposting (i.e., JFK's assassination, the Vietnam War, Reaganomics, 9/11, etc.).

I do not quite have the same luxury in this book. I imagine that I have at least two—but likely more—audiences for this book and this album. On the one hand, I anticipate (hope) that there will be a readership for the *33 1/3 South Asia* series in South Asia. For the most part, I anticipate that these readers will be largely Anglophone, perhaps even Anglophiles, who are already familiar with the Indian music scenes and are also familiar with Hindi cinema (Bollywood) interactions and intersections with these scenes. On the other hand, I anticipate that a larger portion of the readership for this book will be in North America and Europe. Many of these folks might have a passing familiarity with the music and conventions of Indian film, but need a book like this to fill in some of the details to explain why *Dil Chahta Hai* is a landmark album in Hindi cinema. I will not necessarily be able to provide all the necessary cultural and historical knowledge in this book that one might need to fully understand *DCH* as a neophyte (there are lots articles and books that already do this, including some of mine), but I will provide some of the necessary background and resources to at least scratch the surface. As a result, I will at times briefly address some of the cultural-historical landmarks in Indian history that help provide the necessary context for those unfamiliar with India of the 1990s and earlier. I recognize that a book of this length cannot do justice to any of these events, but they will nevertheless be important in understanding some portion of the arguments that I make in this book.

It is also important to situate myself in the story I am about to tell. I am an anthropologist and ethnomusicologist who has taught for two decades in American research universities. For better or worse, my prose in this book will contain the residue of my disciplinary training and the outlook that I have been socialized into as a scholar-teacher of South Asia. My goal is to make this book broadly accessible to insiders and outsiders of Indian film song, but there will be some technical language here and there. I will guide the reader through as we go.

Although this book is the first of the *33 ⅓ South Asia* series to be published, I will not be claiming that *Dil Chahta Hai* is the best or most important film in Hindi cinema. I avoid the facile "Top 25" lists that saturate newspapers and the internet. *Dil Chahta Hai* was not the top grossing film of 2001—that was *Gadar: Ek Prem Katha*—or the best film of 2001—that is arguably the Oscar-nominated *Lagaan* or the family film *Kabhi Khushi Kabhie Gham*. Nor is this SEL's best album—that honor probably goes to *Kal Ho Na Ho* (2003) or *Zindagi Na Milegi Dobara* (2011). *Dil Chahta Hai* is, however, SEL's most important album, a broadly influential film, and transformational soundtrack that ushered in a new sound and approach to music that was adopted by many subsequent music directors in the first decade of the twenty-first century. Ethnomusicologist Gregory Booth (2008) has made a distinction between "Old Bollywood" (i.e., roughly 1947–92, think Naushad, Shankar-Jaikishan, Laxmikant-Pyarelal, R. D. Burman) and "new Bollywood" (roughly 1993–present, think A. R. Rahman, SEL, Pritam, Amit Trivedi) based upon computer-aided production approaches ushered in by digital audio workstations (DAWs) and reduced music production budgets (see also Getter and Balasubrahmaniyan 2008). Within that distinction, therefore, *Dil Chahta Hai* certainly exemplifies new Bollywood as far as production practices are concerned, but a soundtrack that is nevertheless contiguous with the sounds of earlier periods.

The soundtrack introduces a new approach into Indian cinema, an approach that is distinct from A. R. Rahman's approach to layering local and international sounds. In short, *Dil Chahta Hai* evokes what I will call a "rock band aesthetic," that is to say, a collaborative approach to composition and production that utilizes the innovations that DAWs bring with them. They also have a unique identifiable sound that provided an inspiration to Bollywood's fourth generation of music directors. Much of this sound and production aesthetic, I will argue, emerges from the rock-inspired "Indipop" movement of the 1990s, but also shows traces of the experiments of earlier music directors like R. D. Burman, Bappi Lahiri, and Anu Malik. In other words, I want to make the admittedly controversial argument that *Dil Chahta Hai* is the first Bollywood soundtrack composed and produced by a rock band.

Note about Translation and Transliteration

International copyright laws place the burden on the author to acquire the rights to reproduce lyrics. While books released by Indian publishers tend to be more lax about reproducing lyrics without explicit permission, American presses are much more risk-averse and require explicit permission to reproduce lyrics. Thus, as much as I would like to reproduce the complete lyrics of each of the songs in this book's appendix, I was unable to get the necessary permissions. The analysis that follows will include some discussions of lyrics within the limits of American copyright laws (i.e., four lines of text with analysis), but will focus somewhat less upon them than I might otherwise like. Translations of these lyrics can be found in streaming services like Netflix, as well as numerous websites.

All of that said, translations do not always do the work that we'd like—there are a number of poetic ideas that are based upon aesthetic and cultural practices that are difficult to translate precisely and concisely, for example, why "chamkeele din" (sparkling days) sounds like an advertisement. Others are largely untranslatable without a short essay to extract all the nuances, for example, "Pyaar ke ghaat." Nevertheless, one can get the general sense of the meanings of the lyrics, though not a complete picture in commercially available translations.

Finally, a note about transliteration from Devanagari to Roman script. I have chosen to use the most common Roman transliteration that one finds on the internet rather than the academic transliteration (thus, "deewana" and not "dīvānā" for example) to aid non-Hindi/Urdu speakers in following the text as they listen to the songs.

Acknowledgments

When I first proposed this project in 2021, I naively assumed that the worst of the COVID-19 pandemic was behind us and that would all be returning to whatever "normal" is for any individual. I was not prepared for the lingering effects of the pandemic and the new social order that it would bring along with it. As far as this book is concerned, COVID was a blessing in disguise, as it forced me to think about novel approaches to describing this soundtrack and its lasting influences. Another consequence is that my writing slowed down, which had the unintended consequence of enabling me to reach out to people who were involved in the production of the *Dil Chahta Hai* soundtrack through the newly dominant Zoom video meeting platform. I would especially like to thank Vijay Benegal, lead recording and mixing engineer for *DCH* as he answered questions that I had not thought to ask and provided me with great insights into the production of the soundtrack. He also introduced me to other people involved in the project, including Ehsaan Noorani, Loy Mendonsa, and Farhan Akhtar. Authors in this series rarely have the opportunity to talk with the musicians and producers of their albums they write about, so I feel very fortunate to have been able to interview these folks and get their impressions of the soundtrack production and its staying power over the last twenty years. Other people who helped in numerous ways in this project were Shantanu Hudlikar, Clinton Cerejo, and Rhys Sebastian D'Sousa. In Merced, many thanks to Patricia Vergara, Arnold Kim, Paul Gibbons, and Aditi Chandra who provided an important sounding board for the ideas detailed here. Ekta

Kandhway provided assistance with song lyric translations. Thanks also to the series editor Natalie Sarrazin who has been more than patient with each of the delays that I encountered in writing this book. Most importantly, Laura and Gwen were always there when I needed them.

PART I

The Soundtrack

1 *Dil Chahta Hai* Contexts

The various levels of meaning that we might derive from listening to the *Dil Chahta Hai* album emerge from the historical, media, and narrative contexts of the film. In this chapter, I unpack each of these contexts and the ways that this film soundtrack emerges at a particularly important moment in Indian cinematic and musical history, a point in which economic liberalization and a new mediascape have taken hold and urban Indian youth are seeking new models of relating to the world.

Historical Context

The *Dil Chahta Hai* soundtrack emerged out of the social and economic transformations of the 1990s, namely the Liberalization reforms. As a post-colonial state since its Independence in 1947, India's early governments implemented growth plans based in socialist models that favored self-sufficiency and centralized industrial planning that, it was hoped, would help alleviate India's poverty and lead to broad social uplift and spiritual growth. Early Indian governments had an ambivalent relationship with consumerist modes of production, particularly marketing and promotion of products that amplified desires for material goods. This anti-consumerist ideology was reflected in film and media of the 1940s–60s, which depicted consumerism and desires for wealth as an Anglophile holdover from the colonial period.

The general mentality began to change as the planned growth models had uneven outcomes, and shortages of various goods afflicted India's middle classes in the turbulent 1970s and beyond. A prime example of this is the eighteen-month period known as The Emergency (1975–7). India's prime minister, Indira Gandhi, sought to shock the system back on the right track by imposing martial law, restriction of free speech, and implementation of various anti-poverty campaigns that largely doubled down on some of the governmental policies that had dubious merits. The social and economic approach began to unravel somewhat in manufacturing reforms of the 1980s, which made more consumer goods available like cars and televisions. But it is the triple crises of 1991—the first Gulf War, collapse of the Soviet Union, assassination of India's Prime Minister Rajeev Gandhi—that pushed the Indian economy to the brink of collapse. Faced with dwindling foreign currency reserves and imminent default, India's new prime minister, Manmohan Singh, sought and received loans from the World Bank and International Monetary Fund that allowed India's economy to dodge collapse, but with the stipulation that India liberalize its economy. Among other things, this meant that the government divest itself in many industries, reduce social welfare programs, open its economy to foreign investment, and reduce tariffs on imported consumer goods. In the face of two centuries of colonialism, the Indian government had deliberately pursued a self-contained economy. But this desperate need for foreign aid—and the changes necessitated for this aid—created the conditions for dramatic changes in the 1990s. These transformations did not take place overnight and at times faced substantial resistance from social activists.

Changes in technology and media dissemination accompanied social changes in this period. For instance, until the 1980s, televisions were luxury goods that might be shared among several families or an entire village. As manufacturing ramped up, color television was introduced, followed by ad hoc cable TV networks in the 1980s, and television became an increasingly important and prolific medium for television serials (like the *Ramayana*) and a new platform for film dissemination. Foreign satellite broadcasts in the 1990s amplified the presence of television, first as an alternative to cinema halls, then as a medium with distinct content. Almost overnight, many parts of India that may have had access to only a few state-run television channels gained access to myriad satellite channels like CNN, BBC, MTV, and Rupert Murdoch's Star TV. At once there was a need for new local television content and advertising to fill the gaps, which provided new outlets for a new generation of filmmakers and music composers to base their careers.

At the same time, music television channels popped up as a source of inexpensive and popular content for broadcast. Music shows featured music videos in English and Hindi, as well as songs that had been composed for Hindi films. These music television channels facilitated the growth of alternative genres to film songs, including the Urdu language ghazal and Hindipop, that is, Hindi language pop music that draws from international stylistic conventions. This genre later became known as Indipop, the prefix "indi" doing double duty as "Indian" and "independent" (see Kvetko 2005). Artists who had been playing in rock bands in metropolitan clubs in the 1970s onward emerged into a new pop cultural scene that was facilitated by an evolving media landscape. These artist-built careers explicitly branded themselves in opposition to the film song norms of the time. Among other things, this meant that the artists depicted themselves on screen in their music videos, rather than having actors lip-syncing in their place. They consciously deployed international pop and rock styles that were popular among India's urban middle classes. Vocal styles were distinct from the dominant playback singers of the time (Lata Mangeshkar, Asha Bhonsle, Kishore Kumar, Mohammed Rafi) and the new generation of singers who emulated them (e.g., Alka Yagnik, Kumar Sanu). Artists who emerged from this period, including Sonu Nigam, KK, Sukhwinder Singh, Udit Narayan, Alisha, and Usha Uthap, brought new performance practices to the voice that owed as much or more to international rock/pop conventions as they did to Indian classical and folk conventions. Indipop ensembles were anchored by electric guitar, bass, drum sets, and synthesizers and borrowed heavily from the harmonies used in international rock and pop. This is opposed to film song of the time that was based in vocal, lyrical, and instrumental conventions that borrowed heavily from Indian folk and semi-classical traditions, while also including many of these same Western instruments, but used in different ways. Most importantly from Indipop artists' perspective, their musical labor and creative control had been freed from the expectations and deadlines of film producers and directors who deployed songs in service of the film narrative and were ostensibly less interested in the aesthetic properties of the music itself. Television became the most important medium for promoting these new artists, and Indipop videos saturated MTV and other music video channels. Beyond Indipop, ethnomusicologists Chloe Coventry (2013) and Natalie Sarrazin (2024) have written extensively about rock bands in various Indian cities. Very often these bands flew under the radar of Indian media, yet had a powerful influence on local scenes. It is also noteworthy that many current Bollywood musicians and music directors started out in rock bands, including SEL.

The exponential growth of television advertising in the 1980s–90s offered an alternative career trajectory for musicians, that is, composing for media that were not commercial films. Composers working on ad films had the opportunity to take more and different kinds of risks in promoting products—as opposed to the largely conservative approach taken by Hindi film producers. Accordingly, ad films of this period were generally edgier and more future leaning than films of the time as they could be produced more quickly and at much lower cost. It is not surprising that successful ad campaigns on TV caught the attention of film producers, who began to deploy new music directors in films. It makes sense why this would happen: Jingles are important as memorable melodies that have sticky associations with products they are selling. This is precisely the quality that film songs need to have as a herald for new films as they are being released. Most of the current crop of mainstream film song composers, including SEL and A. R. Rahman, cut their teeth on writing advertising music before moving into film. Radio and television audiences were already several steps ahead of mainstream Bollywood music of the time and were simply edgier than the relatively conservative approach of most 1990s mainstream music directors.

Another new technology, audio cassettes, also facilitated the dissemination of new music genres. As ethnomusicologist Peter Manuel has extensively documented in his influential 1993 book *Cassette Culture*, audiocassettes lowered the capital investment and dissemination costs of producing music.

Cassettes allowed much smaller musical production ventures in cities and towns across India, and remained the dominant distribution platform in India well into the first decade of the twenty-first century. It became possible for entrepreneurs in smaller towns and music labels to produce their own music that subverted the homogenizing tendencies of Indian film song that were distributed by HMV via vinyl records. The relatively low production costs of cassettes also facilitated the rise of new urban music labels that not only sought to monetize non-film (i.e., "private") recordings like Indipop (Kvetko 2009) and a new genre called "remix." Remix in an Indian context can mean a few different things, but in the 1990s this largely meant re-recording popular Hindi film songs as a way of doing an end run around the HMV film song monopoly. In some cases, remix albums were shameless copies of film songs, sung by new singers who emulated the original singers. In other cases, remix albums incorporated new beats and new arrangements in ways following Western nomenclature would be described as "covers" rather than "remixes." This remix genre became important for Ehsaan and Loy in their production of the *Dance Masti* series of four albums in their side project, a group called Instant Karma. Inspired by Bally Sagoo's *Bollywood Flashback* album, which rocked the British dance club scene in the mid-1990s, the *Dance Masti* albums largely cover well-known Hindi film songs, with new singers, new arrangers, but largely followed the song forms, melodic and lyrical conventions of the original songs. Well-produced remix videos filled the music television channels of the early 2000s and as I have written in other contexts, they were the source of significant controversy as cultural critics lamented the "plundering" of India's cultural heritage of film songs in order to affix new, often erotic, meanings (Beaster-Jones 2009).

Dil Chahta Hai: The Film

While *Dil Chahta Hai* is widely available on streaming services in 2024, this situation may not always be the case. A brief synopsis might be in order here. Akash (Aamir Khan), Sameer (Saif Ali Khan), and Sid (Akshaye Khanna) have recently graduated from graduated from college in Mumbai (circa 2000) and are now trying to figure out the next stage of their lives. Like most Hindi films, the first half of the narrative focuses upon character development of each of the protagonists and their perspectives as romantic leads. Akash is depicted as the least serious of the three: he has many flings, but does not wish to be tied down by relationships. He essentially views love and romance as a kind of sport. By contrast, Sameer tends toward an earnest affect. In some ways the youngest of the three, he falls head over heels in love with several girls with pretty faces, but also finds himself easily dominated (manipulated) by his love interests. Sid is an artist who is depicted as the most reserved and emotionally mature of the trio. In social interactions, he sits back and observes, often engaged in sketching some aspect of the scene. Their eternal friendship is cemented by a spontaneous road trip to the beaches of Goa, a montage over the title song "Dil Chahta Hai" (The heart wants), where they take in all of the delights afforded to young men of means. Indeed, this part of the film largely reads as a promotional video for Goa Tourism that became the catalyst for many similar road trips for Indian domestic tourists (background song is "Rockin' Goa").

The film narrative pairs each of the boys with a love interest. Akash with Shalini (Priety Zinta), Sameer with Pooja (Sonali Kulkarni), Sid with Tara (Dimple Kapadia). It is the last of these pairings that is the source of the central conflict of the film. An art broker by trade, it is revealed that Tara is significantly older than Sid, a divorced alcoholic with a child from a previous marriage. In short, she is not deemed an appropriate match for the early twenty-something Sid. He keeps his romantic interest in her largely hidden (song: "Kaise Hai Yeh Rut"—What season is this), but Sid's eventual profession of his love for Tara is rejected by his family, and by Tara herself. The bonds of everlasting friendship are shattered, however, when Akash misreads Sid's love interest as merely a quest for sexual experience, which in one pivotal scene Sid dramatically slaps Akash.

The young men go their separate ways. Their wealthy parents each have a different sense of what the next step should be for their sons. Sid goes into artistic isolation at an uncle's cabin to develop his style. Sameer is introduced to Pooja as a potential arranged marriage. Both potential partners profess their disinterest in being subject to arranged marriage—and Pooja is dating another person at this time—but Pooja's beauty beckons to Sameer, and he can barely hide his interest in her. The song, "Woh Ladki Hai Kahan" (Where is that girl) signals the recognition of their mutual romantic interest.

Much of the second half of the film focuses upon the development of the relationship between Akash and Shalini. They had met disastrously at a night club as Akash recited a rehearsed profession of undying love to a girl that he had just met on the dance floor, only to be punched out by the girl's fiancé. This is the setting of the electronic dance number "Koi Kahe Kahta Rahe" (If they say it, let them say it). By extreme coincidence, when Akash's parents send him to Sydney to run a part of their business, Shalini just happens to be seated next to him in first class. They connect a few times for dates in Sydney, and Akash's characteristic stance against romantic love softens in the song, "Jaane Kyon Log Pyar Karte Hai" (I wonder why people fall in love). He comes to realize at a performance of an operatic rendition of *Troilus and Cressida* that he has fallen in love with Shalini, and she with him. At this point, the instrumental melody "Akash's Love Theme" from the background score is added to the soundtrack. Sensing that something is off, Shalini's fiancé arrives in Sydney and spirits her back to Mumbai to be married. This leads to Akash's song "Tanhayee" (Loneliness) as he grapples with the newfound understanding that he is in love with Shalini. It is revealed to Akash that Shalini was orphaned at a young age and had been taken in by a family. She felt a sense of obligation to the son of the family to marry, in spite of the son's abusive tendencies. In true cinematic fashion, Akash shows up at Shalini's wedding to profess his undying love, using the earlier speech, but this time in earnest. Shalini's foster parents come to realize what has happened and release her from any perceived obligation to marry their son. The film flash-forwards six months, presumably after Tara's death, when the boys reunite at the iconic fort in Goa and the "Dil Chahta Hai (Reprise)" in the end credits (see Gehlawat 2017). This being Bollywood, most of the film is flashback that is bookended by hospital scenes of Tara in intensive care for liver failure. The boys are able to overcome their conflict given the circumstances.

Songs in Commercial Indian Cinema

Throughout Indian cinematic history, the conventions of commercial films dictate the overwhelming need for music. Some of this music underscores the film and amplifies or creates the necessary emotional context of any scene. In Hollywood contexts, this would be referred to—and circulated as—as the orchestral score. In India, while background soundtrack is present in virtually every film, it is only rarely distributed on soundtracks and never on its own. Instead, Indian film is famous for incorporating original song compositions by composers known as "music directors," distributing one or more of these songs on radio and television to promote the film in advance of the film release. Done properly, the songs generate a buzz about the film and provide a tantalizing glimpse into some small portion of the film to entice fans to part with some cash to see the film in the theater, or perhaps more likely, to watch a rebroadcast on television or a streaming service. Like any kind of music anywhere, film songs leave traces in individual and social memories, and temporarily linger in the local soundscape to mark a period of time, before being pushed out by the next set of songs. Often, the replay of particular songs is the only remnant of the film once it falls out of the attention of audiences and molders away in a literal or virtual warehouse. Nevertheless, film songs have long been an identifiable and necessary component of Indian cinema and for better or worse, have been the dominant soundtrack of Indian popular culture more generally.

There is a lot of variation in the ways that Hindi film songs are produced, but the basic idea is that a film idea comes into existence (e.g., through a pitch to/by a producer, with particular actors, a general sense of the narrative, etc.) and music director and lyricist are hired for the project by a film producer or director. Typically, the film director narrates the film project to the music director and commissions original music for particular "song situations" in the film that would conventionally require a song. For most films, this means that there are roughly five to eight situations depending upon the narrative needs of the film. As a rule of thumb, conventions dictate that some film genres require more or less than other film genres: action films tend to have fewer song situations than romantic comedies. The songs' melodies and lyrics are composed through the collaboration of the music director(s) and lyricist, pitched to, and green-lighted by the film director and/or producer, sometimes after much negotiation and revision. Individual songs are then recorded in music studios by the musicians and "music programmers," that is, music assistants who otherwise fill in the skeleton of song melody with the flesh and muscle of background melodies, grooves, synthesizer sounds, etc. that make the song recognizable and distinct. Songs are edited and produced through the additional collaboration of sound engineers and music directors to a point that they achieve at least a close to final state from the perspective of the film director/producer. The song recording is then used on the film set, with the actors/actresses lip-syncing the song lyrics to the dance choreography or other movement in the filmic space. This is not to say that the entire song recording is filmed: sometimes songs are expanded, truncated, or interrupted onscreen to fit the needs narrative. Because the focus of the song sequence in the film tends toward visual (i.e., it operates in service to the film narrative rather than standing alone as a song meant for listening), it is common for the recording mix of the film version of the song to be distinct from the soundtrack version of the song. The distributed soundtrack version of a song thus tends to have higher production values and at least to a certain extent, should be able to stand on its own as a discrete composition. In practice, however, songs tend to be associated with the actors who are depicted as singing them, and the emotional contexts in which they appear in the film. Since the music directors, lyricists, and singers are usually rendered invisible, audiences do not see these songs as independent compositions like pop albums in other contexts (hence the Indipop critique of Bollywood).

One consequence of the picturization of film songs is that they always have some visual narrative that accompanies the lyrical and musical narratives. For good films this means that there is mutual support in each of the narratives through the songs. But this is not always the case in practice, in part because film producers often add songs to films to meet the minimum needs of the conventions of films—they see film songs as a necessary evil and do not care so much about how well the song fits the narrative (see Ganti 2012). In other words, mainstream films have had to have songs to have any chance of commercial success (although this attitude has changed fairly recently). Since producing films is a profit-generating enterprise—yet only relatively few films succeed in any given year—film producers tend to be conservative with the music that they green-light for use in a film: they usually stick with what has worked in the past for a conventional set of song situations. Consequently, this means that in any given year, there have been hundreds of songs that fit a formula and are virtually indistinguishable from each other.

Given that there are hundreds of films produced in any given year, and a limited number of possible narrative situations to contain songs, there is a lot of repetition of lyrical, musical, and visual content across the small number of working music directors and lyricists in the industry. Most films in India—and their songs—simply come and go without making any perceivable dent in public consciousness. Their narratives and their music are formulaic and beneath notice. That is to say that the films/songs follow convention too closely, and that there is insufficient novelty to draw the attention of potential listeners/

viewers. This was definitely of the musical landscape of the late 1990s, which has its own distinct and easily recognizable soundprint. It also explains why the most frequently used word to describe *DCH* by music and film reviewers was "fresh."

Musically speaking, film song has always been mediating practice between traditional Indian and transnational conventions, such that film song as a genre developed into its own stylistic fashion—some might say "formula"—that is an original genre bearing the traces of many other genres and their stylistic periods. One reason for this is that Indian music directors have always had translocal perspectives on the music that they create (i.e., they are aware of musical trends) and have tried to find ways to make their songs stand out in an industry that releases hundreds of soundtracks each year, yet still fit within film producer's risk-averse tendencies. The existing song formulas help to explain why reviewer after reviewer noted DCH's youthful sound. Given a new film producer (Ritesh Sidhwani), a new film director (Fahran Akhtar), and new music directors (SEL), the stakes were different and each of them was willing to take some risks that they may not have been afforded if they had established reputations in the film industry.

Film Songs after Liberalization

In the narrative context of the film, the song might be doing several things. In the late 1990s and early 2000s, for example, many films incorporated large group dance numbers that called for multiple singers (for each of the film stars on screen) and bombastic danceable music that foregrounded percussion in the mix. These kinds of dance numbers often became the primary representative of the film in the television and radio marketing campaigns. The same films might also include several songs shot on the hero(ine) that might, for instance, provide insights into the interior mental-emotional state of the character at that time, illustrate the personalities of the characters, create an opportunity for on-screen flirtation, or simply introduce new characters. Other songs create the opportunity for characters to represent religious piety and morality, assert the depth of friendships, mourn the loss of a relationship, demonstrate resolve in a difficult situation, and so forth. Songs are consciously designed for audiences to generate relationships, empathize, and otherwise identify themselves with the heroes and heroines of the film. As a result, villains do not get songs, although antiheroes and other morally flawed characters might get to sing.

Music director A. R. Rahman blasted into the scene with the songs of his 1992 Tamil film *Roja* having been dubbed into Hindi, and his subsequent films of the 1990s, including *Bombay* (1995), *Dil Se* (1998), and *Taal* (1999) (see Sarrazin 2008). These superhit films helped to unveil the tastes of a youth that had been exposed to international musics via music television channels. Rahman effectively demonstrated that there was a market for new voices and a new sound aesthetic in Indian cinema. This was a decade in which dominant music directors R. D. Burman and Laxmikant of the Laxmikant-Pyarelal duo passed away and new music directors like Jatin-Lalit, Anu Malik, Raamlaxman and others continued in their footsteps by creating huge soundtracks prominently featuring violin sections and vocal choruses, and continuity with the same kinds of solo voices derived from the sounds of earlier generations of playback singers.

There were at least two distinct sounds of Hindi film soundtracks of the 1990s, one that followed directly from existing musical lineages, the other self-consciously disrupting earlier practices through new studio techniques, songs forms, and voices. In this book, I am arguing that SEL provided a third approach, one that started with Dil Chahta Hai and became the template for a new kind of sound derived from a rock band aesthetic that ultimately became a millennial landmark.

2 Shankar-Ehsaan-Loy's Rock Band Aesthetic

The soundtrack to *Dil Chahta Hai* (*DCH*) is fundamentally a creation of the modern recording studio, most notably the digital audio workstation (DAW). DAWs came into regular use in India in the 1990s and they operate as a hybrid of the aural and visual representations of sound. In this context, tracks are recorded by individual musicians in sound-treated studio spaces and cut, mixed, adapted, transformed, and layered into a single composition on a computer. From this production perspective, and as these technologies became ubiquitous, there is no great difference between *DCH* and other recordings that have been produced over the last twenty-five years inside and outside of India, even if some of the tools of the trade have become more sophisticated. All of the songs were all recorded with a click track, they used compressors, digital effects, and conventional sound recording practices. To this extent, SEL followed common recording best practice. What I am arguing here, however, is that the production of *DCH* deploys a *rock band* aesthetic in ways that were qualitatively different from other music directors of the day. What do I mean by a "rock band aesthetic" and how is *DCH* different from contemporaneous productions?

By a rock band aesthetic, I mean that SEL compositions are predisposed to have several characteristics which make the sound of their compositions distinct from other music directors of their era. This distinct sound emerges from their individual musical experiences and production practices as a band. Many of these tendencies draw from their intersecting influences in Indian classical, rock, jazz, and blues musics. The identifying characteristics that I identify below include riff-based songs, the use Western chordal harmony, a rock ensemble that avoids the use of string orchestras, rock song forms (verse-chorus-bridge form), the sounds of electric guitar, backing vocals (as opposed to vocal chorus), a jam-based compositional approach, and a distinct sound aesthetic. Let us consider each of these points in turn as a way to build an argument about the SEL sound and how it departs from the conventional sound of the era. Some of this gets a little bit technical—I am a musicologist after all—but I hope to keep it comprehensible for lay readers.

Riff-Based Compositions

As a starting point, many SEL compositions tend to be based around a recognizable riff, a short repeated melodic phrase that are usually recognizable elements of the song on their own. Often these are guitar riffs (opening riff to "Woh Ladki," "Kaisi Hai Yeh Rut," "Dil Chahta Hai—reprise," "Rockin' Goa"), other times they are in the bass ("Dil Chahta Hai," "Tanhayee") or other melodic instruments (the fiddle and flutes in "Woh Ladki"). These riffs operate as the base of the song and are often the foundation on which the rest of the song is built. In addition to the electric guitar sound generally, this characteristic of riff-basis distinguishes SEL from A. R. Rahman (who also has a rock band background), inasmuch as Rahman tends to replicate drones through the use of layered synthesizer pads and ostinato (repeated) rhythms in his compositions. By contrast, SEL tend to use distinctive rhythmic-melodic approaches (riffs) in a great many of their compositions, both in *DCH* and beyond. These characteristics, I will later argue, led music critics and fans to refer to *DCH* as a "fresh" approach to film song and the "Millennial soundtrack."

Chordal Harmony

Beyond riff-based compositions, another component of the rock band aesthetic is SEL's approach to chordal harmony that is comparable to many international rock and jazz musicians. That is to say that most of their songs have a chord progression of some sort that draws from Western conventions of harmonic tension and release in and through the relationships of chords to each other in time. Very frequently the harmonic bases of their songs are drawing explicitly from rock, blues, and jazz—most commonly, the IV-V-I blues chord progression. This also means that chordal instruments, especially keyboards, bass, and guitars, are in the foreground of the mix and are a critical part of the sonic texture of their songs in ways that are distinct from most of their predecessors. Music directors in earlier periods, and even most of SEL's contemporaries of the time, used chordal instruments in their orchestras, and even incorporated chord progressions. Yet these instruments tended to be hidden in the mix and relatively easy to miss even with repeated listening. What tended to be at the front of more conventional Hindi film song contexts of the late 1990s were Indian drums (e.g., dhol, tabla) and melodic instruments (e.g., voice, choir, violins, etc.). Bass and chordal instruments tended to be shunted to the back of the mix. In addition, the *DCH* soundtrack also deploys extended harmonies, such as 7ths and 9ths that were largely unused in Hindi language films up to this point. In short, chordal harmony is an integral part of their compositions and a critical component of their overall sound, which I discuss in more detail below.

Ensemble

Like other music directors in the history of Indian cinema, SEL use an eclectic variety of instruments in their ensembles as a part of their regular sound pallet, depending upon the needs for the given composition (e.g., the film settings). However, their core ensemble is functionally a rock band: voice, guitar, keyboards, bass, drums. In addition to keyboards, Loy often handles bass and drums through synth programming, though for more complex compositions they may bring in a bassist like Karl Peters (who is among the most sought-after bassists in Mumbai's jazz scene) or a drummer like Taufiq Qureshi (a prolific studio drummer and Zakir Hussain's younger brother), both of whom worked on this particular soundtrack. Even when programming the drums for a given song, SEL are more likely to draw from Western three or four beat meters rather than Indian folk or classical meters (i.e., *tala*).

Unlike other music directors of the 1990s and early 2000s that foreground the virtuosic, high-flying unison string sections, SEL tend to use the orchestral string section (e.g., violins, violas, cellos) sparingly. When they do use strings (or synthesized string sounds), these parts are in their lower registers and harmonized rather than in unison. In *DCH*, strings are only used briefly in "Kaisi Hai" and "Tanhayee," and are harmonized in both cases, which is similar to A. R. Rahman's approach to strings in his compositions. A good contrast here is Jatin-Lalit's contemporaneous soundtrack to *Kabhi Khushi Kabhie Gham* (2001), which heavily leans on percussion, choral passages, and unison strings to accompany the voices in ways that draw heavily from the established practices of earlier music directors, particularly Laxmikant-Pyarelal, albeit within the context of the studio/DAW practice described above (see Booth 2008).

The use of a choir, or lack thereof, is another distinguishing feature of SEL compositions: the mixed vocal chorus singing vocables (sounds without lexical meaning) in unison is a characteristic of so many Bollywood family films of the 1990s, to the point of ubiquity. Yet these are largely absent in SEL compositions. SEL instead take a different tack to using voices by recording tight, stacked vocal harmonies from vocalists who are better characterized as backing singers in the Western style than as Bollywood choral voices in conventional film songs. The timbres and qualities of sound of the background singers are different in SEL compositions because they are mixed differently: they are not being used as a chorus where all of the voices are melded together into a single instrument, but as discrete voices contributing a different portion of a vocal harmony. This created a sound of backup singing reminiscent of Western artists like Steely Dan, the Doobie Brothers, or Hall and Oats distinct from other Indian music directors who recorded choirs in unison. The use of backing singers is present throughout *DCH* but is especially noticeable in the title track and its reprise. The exception that proves the rule here is the quasi-African sounding chorus in "Jaane Kyon" that is recorded very differently from the backing vocal approach in the other songs on the soundtrack.

Solo Vocalists

Over the course of their respective careers, SEL and A. R. Rahman have experimented with different vocal timbres in their compositions. Their success with this approach has meant that the sound of Hindi film songs has undergone significant shifts in the twenty-first century—from the traditional Lata Mangeshkar, Asha Bhosle, Kishore Kumar, Mohammed Rafi timbres for female and male singers to a different sound altogether. Some of this was foreshadowed by the qualified success of Indipop as pop genre independent from cinema (see Kvetko 2005) and the calculated absorption of Indipop voices into Hindi film songs. Of course, this did not happen overnight and in the case of *DCH* one might reasonably argue that voices of Alka Yagnik and Kavita Krishnamurthy are cast in the Lata-Asha mold, which is one reason why their songs remain among the most popular on the soundtrack. Nevertheless, the male voices in the soundtrack bear the traces of Indipop vocal approach, a hybrid of pop and *filmi* sound.

Electric Guitar

SEL songs tend to feature electric guitar in the foreground of the recording mix. Usually this is Ehsaan himself playing, but at times other guitarists might be brought to the studio for other kinds of guitar sound, particularly acoustic guitar. In the title track, for example, Ehsaan's lead break is a clear and indelible imprint of his presence on the soundtrack. There are any number of other songs across their repertoire that similarly feature electric guitar in a variety of timbres (i.e., with distortion, chorus, fuzz, reverb/delay, etc.). The timbre of Ehsaan's guitar points to his extensive practice and training at the Musician's Institute in Los Angeles in the mid-1980s and his interactions with other up-and-coming guitarists of that period and beyond. The guitar sound in *DCH* thus created a novel sound space for experimentation in ways that interestingly parallel R. D. Burman's approach of the 1960s–70s.

Song Form

Like instrumentation, SEL experiment song forms in the compositions. These are likely to draw as much from the verse-chorus-bridge form in international popular musics as they do from the *mukhda-antara*—roughly refrain-verse—form of Hindi film songs (or as I will show in the next chapter, some amalgam of these forms since they are not mutually exclusive). Over the years, SEL moved increasingly in the direction of "verse-chorus" song forms. However, in the case of *DCH*, they heeded Javed Akhtar's advice to stick with the mukhda-antara form, which would be familiar to most film song audiences. In this form, the *mukhda* (lit. face) of the composition functions as the hook—it is usually the starting melody and lyrics of the song and the most frequently repeated. The *antara*, by contrast, functions much like the verse of a rock song and differs melodically from the *mukhda* and tends toward more lyrical exposition, albeit with less catchy melodies. That said, they did play with the melodic form to create some song forms that create a hybrid between these approaches. Most notable in SEL songs is the inclusion of a "bridge" or "middle eight" in many of their songs, a song section present in a large number of international rock songs that brings in a harmonic contrast that is distinct from the verse and chorus.

Compositional Approach

Members of SEL suggest that each song they write comes into existence in a different way from the composer, arranger, programmer relationships of earlier Indian cinema. Some of these songs come into existence through a process of jamming together to see what musical ideas emerge organically. Different compositions might emerge from a particular melodic, harmonic, or rhythmic idea, for example, or emerge from an adoption or mediation of a particular musical style like country, reggae, a *qawwali*, or *bhajan*. There is thus a similarity of the compositional models described by heavy metal scholar Deena Weinstein (2000) that parallels rock band practices in other parts of the world. Given that compositions are generated and adapted in the studio, these ideas are recorded and refined in a DAW, layered, added to, experimented with, and so forth. In the case of *DCH*, SEL's approach to songwriting incorporated each of these elements, as Javed Akhtar was in the room with them as they composed the soundtrack. More than anything else, however, Shankar, Ehsaan, and Loy describe themselves as a band in many interviews, including my interviews with them later in this book.

The SEL Sound

The sound aesthetic is the most ephemeral component of SEL soundtracks, something that is distinct and recognizable element of their recordings, yet also the most difficult to describe in layperson's terms. The sound of any composition emerges from the thousands of decisions that are made in the process of recording an album, from the vocal inflections to be used, the kind of groove that develops between percussion instruments, to the sound frequencies to emphasize or move to the background, the ways that multitrack recordings of a drum set or backing vocalist will be combined at a particular moment in a song to give it a complete sound, to the kinds of musical effects that are added to each individual track in the studio (e.g., reverb or digital delay, filters, compression, gating, etc.). Many of these decisions are made by SEL themselves, but these choices frequently emerge from negotiations between musicians and sound engineers. In this case, Vijay Benegal, a veteran of hard rock albums, worked as the lead recording and mixing engineer and he certainly brought his own aesthetic to the final product.

In short, I would like to emphasize the characteristics described above for many, but not all of SEL's compositions. Some songs are self-consciously "Indian" in their orientation—that is, that they draw explicitly from Indian semi-classical, folk, or devotional styles that do not necessarily have chord progressions, rock instrumentation, or experimental song forms. Yet SEL's canon of hits is more likely to have some or most of the characteristics noted above. Band members stress the experimental aesthetic and eclecticism of the group—that none of their hits sound like their other hits. They have a recognizable sound, but it is not simply on stylistic bases. Instead, it emerges from a confluence of their musical experiences, coupled with a set of musical practices, their rock band aesthetic, that make their songs readily identifiable even on the first listen.

3 The Rock Band Aesthetic in *Dil Chahta Hai*

As I discussed in the previous chapter, SEL deploys a rock band aesthetic in *Dil Chahta Hai* that became a model for later music directors in the first decades of the twenty-first century. To a greater or lesser extent, these characteristics of the rock band aesthetic are present in each of the compositions on this soundtrack. In this chapter, I discuss each of the songs, pointing out some of the rock band components one might hear with a close listen. Each song description will open with a translation of the *mukhda*, a musical term that is derived from Indian classical music but denotes something a bit different in a film song context. It is usually comprised of the first lyrics of any given song, a repeated melody, and serves both as the song title and the melodic hook. As such, the *mukhda* is typically the most important and memorable part of any given film song and serves a critical role in the popularity of the song, the soundtrack, and the case of title tracks, the film. Given the prominence of the *mukhda* in the film song, it is not surprising that film producers in the 1990s onwards aggressively recruited television and radio jingle composers for their film projects. In the case of SEL, Ehsaan was recruited by producer Mukul Anand on the strength of a late 1990s Pepsi commercial to compose the music for his film *Dus*. Ehsaan then brought Loy and Shankar on board. As he comments in his interview chapter, "the rest is history, literally, like it was fated to happen."

Given the space constraints of this volume, I will not provide an exhaustive analysis of each track, but instead point to the song's context in the film, the ways in which one might hear SEL's rock band aesthetic in action, along with other dimensions of the songs that became highly influential for Hindi film song composers in the subsequent two decades.

Track 1—"Dil Chahta Hai" (Title Track)

Mukhda
Dil chahta hai, kabhi na beete chamkeele din
Dil chahta hai, hum na rahein kabhi yaaron ke bin

[The heart wants these sparkling days to never end
The heart wants that never be without friends]

Like other films, the title track has several purposes: most importantly, it advertises the film, which is similar to Laxmikant-Pyarelal's 1980s–90s practice and the prevailing practices of later music directors. It is also tied to an iconic scene in the film—the road trip to Goa in one of their parent's convertible Mercedes sedan. Beyond its use in the film, cultural critics have pointed to the title track as the consummate holiday song, "Goa became synonymous with *Dil Chahta Hai* that people visiting the state would play songs of this film while driving with their friends. Even the fort three of them chill at became a popular tourist spot for all friends" (Devki Vats 2020). One newspaper article went so far as to argue that the film singlehandedly saved Goa tourism in the aftermath of the September 11 terrorist attacks. One might reasonably speculate that this song alone bears a significant amount of responsibility for the film's success as an unintended jingle for Goan Tourism more generally. The title song eschews a number of expectations of Hindi cinema, perhaps most poignantly, lip syncing and dance by the actors which was unusual, but not unheard of in this period of Hindi cinema. It is possible that this film set the trend, as many future film directors dispensed with lip-syncing in the 2010s and song montages became common. While it is the first song on the soundtrack, it is the second song in the film, which also heightens its musical impact. In the film, the musical bridge fades in after a short reflective sequence of the characters sitting on a rock wall at Chapora Fort looking out to the seascape in front of them. Akash and Samir express their desire to keep having this kind of moment in the future, laced with Sid's premonition that their lives may lead them on different paths. The boys express their undying friendship, but the music bridge reinforces the uncertainty of the life ahead of them:

> Usko jaana kidhar hai
> Jo waqt aaye, jaane kya dikhaaye
>
> [Who knows where one is supposed to go
> Who knows what the future will reveal]

The music of this song has a well-known origin story. Shankar had an insight while brushing his teeth during their composer retreat. SEL had been planning to use this particular bass line for "Jaane Kyon," but Shankar realized that the lyrics "Dil Chahta Hai" fit over the bass rhythm and ran into the rehearsal space, toothbrush in hand, at which point they dropped everything else and finished composing the song. Farhan Akhtar, the film director, noted that he was unsure about some of the lyrics of the song, particularly "Chamkeele Din" (sparkling days). His concern was that the lyrics sounded like an advertisement for laundry detergent. The phrase was certainly unusual: they came at a time when the lyrical lexicon in Hindi language songs was fairly limited. That said, there are a number of unusual words and phrases in the songs of this soundtrack, a part of the overall design that makes it sound fresh, even as it reintroduced some lyrical imagery from earlier periods of film song (see Akhtar and Kabir 2005).

Musically speaking, there are several features of "Dil Chahta Hai" that make it stand out from other film songs of the time. The first thing one might notice is the background vocalists in the intro and during the song's chorus, like the rising "oh oh oh oh" vocals—as distinct from the mukhda of the song. The background vocalists sing in tight, close-miked harmony that is dissonant at times, a rarity in film songs. This use of harmonized background vocalists is distinct from the use of the unison choral approach developed by Laxmikant-Pyarelal and deployed by many music directors of the 1990s. The mixed unison choral approach appears with great effect by Jatin-Lalit in the family film soundtracks that were in vogue at the time, such as *Dilwale Dulhania Le Jayenge* (1995) and *Kabhi Khushi Kabhie Gham* (2001).

A second distinctive feature is the electric guitar solo. Electric guitars with various timbres have been used in Hindi film songs from the earliest days of the genre, and the guitar is certainly an important characteristic of many songs. Ehsaan's style of playing the guitar in the title track, however, is something new. Its aggressive, overdriven sound points directly to an international rock guitar style in which Ehsaan was well-versed given his experience at the Musician's Institute in LA in the 1980s. The first hint we get of his guitar sound is in the pre-chorus (lyrics "Din Din Bhar"), then a more expansive rock-style lead break into this track that is completely unlike any other previous music director in Hindi film.

A third feature of the rock band aesthetic in the title track is covert mediation of rock song form into a conventional Indian film song form. One could point to the lyrical sections of the song and argue that it follows the usual pattern of the mukdha-antara form and be correct. Turning the song on its head, however, the melodic form sounds suspiciously like a rock song, with a pre-chorus (lyrics "Din Din Bhar") leading into the mukhda (lyrics "Dil Chahta Hai") followed by a chorus ("oh oh oh oh"). After the guitar lead break, there is a bridge (lyrics "Kaisa Ajab") followed by the chorus. All of this to say that the title track captures a point of transition from traditional song forms into the verse-chorus style that heralds many of SEL's later songs.

There is a lot more to note about this track, including the lack of long musical interludes that characterize other film songs of this period, the avoidance of a string section, the programmed rock beat, the subtle but present chord progression with Loy flashing some dissonant extended chords in the synths, the use of synthesizers as synthesizers rather than as a substitute for other instruments, and so forth. Most importantly, however, all the elements combine both to create a great song and to expand the sonic and timbral scope of possibility for future Hindi film songs.

Track 2—Jaane Kyon

Mukhda
Jane kyon log pyar karte hain
Jane kyon vo kisi pe marte hain

[I wonder why people fall in love
I wonder why people pine for one another]

Each of the male leads gets a song to explore their character's relationship to the female character they are associated with, and with their individual relationship to love in the abstract. Akash and Shalini's song is "Jaane Kyon Log Pyar Karte Hai" (Why do people fall in love). Shot in Sydney, Australia, this conversational song follows from the long history of Hindi love songs shot in picturesque foreign locations. The exoticness of the location is evoked as much in sound as in image from the start: a didgeridoo is prominent at the beginning, one among the most distinctive sounds ever used for a Hindi film song. Reviewers and audiences often comment that this song was their very first exposure to the instrument. Given the shooting location, the instrumental choice and its distinct timbre are appropriate given the instrument's association with Indigenous Australia. Similarly, the breathy, flute-like synthesizer melody that fills in the gaps of Udit Narayan's vocal line also evokes a kind of playful Australian folk sound.

The first half of the song is based around a drone, descending bass slides, instrumental melody on a santur, and rhythmic vamp at a fast walking tempo that is punctuated by ankle bells (*ghoonghroo*). The delivery of the vocal melody is at once playful and flirtatious. Udit Narayan voicing Aamir Khan asks, perhaps facetiously, why do people fall in love? The melodic line gradually moves up the scale as the protagonist seemingly finds all kinds of faults with love, but up to a point of exaggeration—at a prominent moment asking "Zehr Kyun Zindagi Men Bharte Hain" (Why do people fill life with poison) to goad his walking partner to respond.

And respond she does. Alka Yagnik's soaring voice cuts across the rhythm—and the artifice—that Akash infuses with his superficial perspective on love. It is worth noting here that the sound of Alka's voice and her semi-classical melodic delivery is perhaps the most traditional sound in this entire soundtrack, given that the melody, high register, and the timbre of voice itself harken back to Lata Mangeshkar's long dominance in Hindi cinema and conventional representations of love in Hindi cinema. Beneath Udit's melodic vocal play, there is no harmonic movement, just a vamp: this is a monochromatic, straw man picture of love that Akash paints. But SEL do not let us remain in the black and white: Loy's synth harmonies provide a pad beneath Alka's voice that transforms the superficial monochrome to a rich color. The synthesizer adds vibrancy and urgency to the earnestness of Shalini's perspective: "Pyar Bin Jine Men Rakkha Kya Hai. Pyar Jis ko Nahin Vo Tanha Hai" (What is the point of living without love? Without love there is only loneliness). The deployment of the word tanha (loneliness) in the lyrics here nicely foreshadows Akash's song "Tanhayee" (loneliness) later in the soundtrack.

In spite of the instrumentation and quasi-African chorus singing vocable syllables, this is the most conventional song on the soundtrack. Perhaps for that reason, and the voices of Alka Yagnik and Udit Narayan, it is also one of the most popular tracks on the album. It won an award for playback singing and was nominated for several other awards.

Track 3—Woh Ladki Hai Kahan

Mukhda
Jisse dhoondta hoon main har kahin
Jo kabhi mili mujhe hai nahin

Mujhe jiske pyaar par ho yakeen
Woh ladki hai kahan

[The one I am looking for everywhere
The one whom I have never found
The one whose love I can trust
Where is that girl?]

The music video is cute. It is set in a classic art deco movie theater in Mumbai as the location of a date between Sameer and Pooja. The song title is announced by a film poster at the beginning of the video (while they are presumably in the lobby), then while they are watching the film, takes them through several eras of Hindi cinema with a unified dance hook (roughly described, a bird flapping its wings). Choreographer and future film director Farah Khan won a Filmfare award for her dance choreography on this song, but credits her assistant, Geeta Kapur, with development of the dance move (INS 2020). One film critic noted that "In my movie-watching life, *Dil Chahta Hai* was the first time actors were changing costumes and locations not because they were vamping while hopping from a Dutch meadow to a Swiss hillside, but because their debate takes place over the course of many days, weeks, and months" (Balial 2022). In the lyrics, Pooja (voiced by Kavita Krishnamurthy) implores Sameer (voiced by Shaan) to keep looking for this fairy (pari), elf (apsara), nymph of his dreams—a set of unusual poetic images that made their way into the song by way of Javed Akhtar's pen. She initially denies that she might be this girl but goes on to accept that she might be this person after all.

The most distinctive element of this song is the Irish-inspired riff that separates the vocal sections of the song. In interviews, SEL say that they were listening to Afro-Celtic music on the way to their retreat to compose the soundtrack, which in turn influenced SEL's use of fiddles/tin whistles (mixed with bansuri) in this track. Moreover, the tap shoe dance rhythm does not receive much notice, but I have not heard this sound in any other Hindi film song. The song also uses a blues IV-V-I progression and a country guitar sound that foreshadows "Slow Angrez" on the 2013 *Bhaag Milkha Bhaag* soundtrack. Accordingly, it fits well within the rock aesthetic while also doing double duty as a film song.

Track 4—"Kaisi Hai Yeh Rut"

Mukhda
Kaisi hai ye rut ki jis men phul ban ke dil khilen
Ghul rahe hain rang sare ghul rahi hain khushbuen
Chandni jharne ghatayen, geet barish titliyan
Ham pe ho gaye hain sab meherban

[What season is this in which the heart blossoms like a flower?
All colors and fragrances are blending together
Moonlight, waterfalls, and clouds, songs, rain, and butterflies
They all bestow grace on us]

I must admit that this has never been one of my favorite songs, in large part because the beauty of the music and lyrics is overshadowed by the now awkward CGI used in the video track. The picturization innocuously begins with Sid beginning to paint Tara's portrait a little over an hour in the film without lip-syncing the words. About a minute and a half into the song, at the first *antara*, there is one of the very few key modulations (i.e., change of fundamental pitch) that one hears up to this point in Hindi film songs, along with some nice extended harmony. But the picturization skips to a fantasy space. The visual and lyrical imagery come into alignment with each other as Sid, now clothed in a white kurta pajama, paints next to a river. The overly soft camera lens, oversaturated colors, and Sid's lip-syncing lead into an unfortunately cheesy image of the actor atop a glowing moon in the middle of the ocean with a dolphin jumping nearby. It is difficult to unsee this image, even if it is representative of Sid's artistic and sensitive interiority. It is noteworthy that the other two love songs are duets, but "Kaisi Hai" is solo voice: it is a subtle representation of unrequited love. Film director Farhan Akhtar took a significant risk in making a divorcee a love interest for one of the lead characters and while it would have been nice for Tara to have a song, it probably would have been too much for some audiences.

With close listening, away from the video, the song reveals its beauty—a sweet and tuneful vocal melody, along with an unusually vivid natural imagery in the lyrics and some unusual word choices propels the song forward. The lyrical structure of the song is somewhat of a throwback to an earlier era—not quite a *ghazal*, but *ghazal*-like in the way that it brings back the *mukhda* at the end of longer phrases in ways that are resonant of a *qafia* (concluding word or refrain). This, in addition to the xylophone-like arpeggios that ripple through the song, double-time ride cymbal in a jazz style, guitar with chorus pedal playing a slower arpeggiated figure, over which floats Srinivas's voice like a paper boat on a swiftly moving stream. Even if the picturization might be awkward some twenty years later, the musical and lyrical imagery carry the song forward. This is the most poetic of the songs on the soundtrack, very much a Javed Akhtar composition. Naveen Kumar's flute solos also propels this song forward. The pastoral associations of the flute (*bansuri*) in Hindi film song should be noted in passing: the sound represents unspoiled nature in mountain spaces, particularly when accompanied by reverb or delay, as well as associations with the god Krishna and romantic love. This is one of the few songs on the soundtrack that incorporate a string section, but strings are harmonized in the lower registers and relegated to the background of the mix.

The song form of "Kaise Hai" is quite similar to a jazz song, even though it is lyrically in the mukdha-antara form. Indeed, the second antara sounds like a return to the bridge that frequently takes place jazz ballads. This fact, coupled with the harmonic modulation that comes along with it, is very subtle, but quite unusual for a film song. The ending of the song with background vocals in harmony reminds the listener that they are still in the middle of a rock band composition, while the flute keeps us firmly anchored in a cinematic musical frame. It is noteworthy that this dream sequence is consistently listed as one of the favorites of the musicians themselves, even though it lagged a bit in popularity on the soundtrack more generally.

Track 5—"Koi Kahe Kehta Rahe"

Mukhda
Koi kahe kehata rahe kitana bhi hamako divaana
Ham logoan ki ṭhokar mean hai yah zamana

[If they say how crazy we are, let them say it
The older generation's opinion does not matter to us]

This first song in the film, "Koi Kahe" is set in a crowded dance club in Mumbai, a graduation party celebrating the end of the college chapters in their lives. Akash, Sameer, and Sid are hanging out with their classmates and goofing around. Akash is avoiding Deepa, a girl who has a crush on him. Sid is focused upon a picture he is drawing and seemingly oblivious to the scene. As Sameer and his girlfriend begin arguing, Sid rouses himself from his project and announces, "Finished." He had been drawing the image of a woman in another part of the club. And so we're introduced to Shalini, who immediately catches Akash's eye. He moves to the club's stage, interrupting the DJ with a speech that leads into the song. Akash is voiced by the singer Shankar Mahadevan, Sameer by Shaan, Sid by KK. Of the three voices, Shaan's youthful sound best approximates what we might imagine as Sameer's singing voice, and connects later with "Woh Ladki"; the other two singers' voices are a little less well connected to their actors. Like the other songs on the soundtrack, one can hear the palpable sound of Indipop in their vocal approach and a turn to another set of sonic possibilities. The resulting multistar, large-scale dance routine (also choreographed by Farah Khan) is very much an artifact of this period of Indian cinema: song sequences set in nightclubs and discotheques have a long history in Hindi film. As such, the picturization is relatively conventional, even if the choice to create a techno song for a Hindi film song was novel. The song is a standard mukhda-antara form, and thus begins with the hook and song title. But a line of the hook also deserves some attention, as it encapsulates the film as a whole, what Farhan Akhtar is trying to convey more generally with *Dil Chahta Hai*.

> Ham hain naye, andaz kyon ho purana
> [We are the new generation, why should our style be old-fashioned?]

"Koi Kahe" is, at its heart, a youth anthem, and the setting of a graduation party is hardly accidental. It calls out antiquated generational ideologies and calls for a new youthful outlook. As music journalist Narendra Kusnur pointed out to me in conversation, the song *performs* the new generational order of Javed Akhtar's lyrics. Inasmuch as *Dil Chahta Hai* has been dubbed "the Millennial soundtrack," this song operates as the cornerstone of Millennial values—a generation that did not experience the tribulations and austerities of India's earlier economic eras and had a genuinely optimistic outlook on their future. Anything is possible in the post-Liberalization moment; one just has to change their attitude. This is not to say that these values were above critique, as several film reviewers pointed to *DCH* as a film that represents the values and problems of the super affluent, not the common man.

The singers are performing in unison, which distinguishes this song from the others on the soundtrack. After an introductory section, a snare drum rhythm leads into the groove. This is a groove-based song, with the bass line anchoring it, along with a techno-disco programmed electronic drums and intermittent tabla samples. Like other dance songs, the pace seems slightly ahead of the beat, creating rhythmic tension. In the musical interludes the bass drops out leaving four-on-the-floor bass drum. One thing that I noticed after many listenings is the cowbell playing a 3–2 *son clave* rhythm, one of the delightful intersections of SEL's musical influences. To my ear, the ending of the song is flat, and like so many film songs, it is somewhat longer than it should be. But it fits the needs of the director and picturization for the film narrative.

"Koi Kahe" has had an outsized influence in the history of film song. It may be difficult to remember given the broad sweep of Bollywood film songs over the last two decades, but this song functionally introduced techo-EDM into the stream of stylistic possibilities for Hindi film songs, to the extent that this EDM style became ubiquitous in the industry. It was widely copied by subsequent music directors. This is not to say that disco-influenced dance songs were new—these had been present as far back as the 1970s with R. D. Burman songs and continued into the 1980s with Bappi Lahiri songs. Nor was this the first electronica song in Indian—the so-called "remix" movement that adapted older film songs into new dance-inspired styles was well underway since the 1990s following Bally Sagoo's *Bollywood Flashback* in the UK that became wildly popular in Indian metropolitan dance clubs. Indeed, Loy and Ehsaan belonged to the group Instant Karma that had produced several very popular albums. Rather, the influence of "Koi Kahe" stems from being a techno-dance song composed as an original to stand on its own in a film soundtrack. Interviews with Loy and Ehsaan emphasized this fact.

Track 6—Akash's Love Theme

This song has an unusual history. Michael Harvey is an Australian composer who has worked extensively as a composer and musician since the 1970s. He was approached by the film's producer (Ritesh Sidhwani) to compose a short opera for the film that they knew would be a component of the film narrative, namely the Akash-Shalini love story. Harvey wrote a series of six short pieces (one to two minutes each) that would make up the opera depicted in the film. The original composition came to approximately twelve minutes, then was further cut down to six minutes for the film. The overture to the opera ultimately became "Akash's Love Theme" in the soundtrack, and indeed accompanies Akash as a leitmotif, or a repeated melodic idea associated with a character or idea, that has some prominence in the film. As I have noted in other venues, the inclusion of portions of the background score in the song soundtrack is highly unusual in Hindi films, and yet ARR had done something similar in the soundtrack for *Lagaan* and his later soundtrack to *Swades* (Beaster-Jones 2017). The tricky thing that Harvey notes here is that he had to compose a theme that would be accessible to an Indian audience of hundreds of millions, very few of whom would know the conventions of European opera. He thus decided to write in a "commercial" style reminiscent of late nineteenth-century Puccini and Massenet compositions, composers who were well known for writing beautiful and engaging melodies for lay audiences to Western art music. The libretto (lyrics) for the piece was in French and one of the singers in the soundtrack was picturized onscreen. Harvey composed and recorded the pieces, which were approved by the production team, then adjusted to fit the filming in the State Theater in Sydney. All told, it took Harvey just a couple of days to compose and record these operatic moments in Sydney, which he then passed on to the film director. It is notable that Harvey had no contact with SEL in the production of the piece, even though portions of the opera were included in the final version of the background score.

This two-minute track deploys a full chamber orchestra in the Western classical style. It has a clear musical theme that gradually develops a thicker texture of strings, horns, and brass by the end. It is a lovely melody that follows Western harmonic conventions, although its presence in this soundtrack is a bit incongruous.

Track 7—"Tanhayee"

Mukhda
Tanhayee
Dil ke raste men kaisi thokar main ne khayi
Tute khwab sare ek mayusi hai chhayi
Har khushi so gayi

[Loneliness
I stumbled so badly on the path of love
All my dreams lie shattered, there is despair all around
Every joy has fallen into slumber]

This is the final song in the film narrative proper, about two-and-a-half hours into the film. After a dinner with Rohit, Shalini, and her uncle, Akash is reminded both of their first meeting and that Shalini is engaged. Rohit invites Akash to their wedding, but Akash once again professes not to believe in love. In his last interaction with Shalini, she notes that Akash did not see the opera singer as his love interest, as he had joked in the theater, but instead saw someone else. Akash walks away with the chunky bass groove of "Tanhayee" fading in. In the "Making of Dil Chahta Hai" short film included with the DVD, actor Saif Ali Khan notes that Tanhayee is an "angry sad song… because not all grief is poetic, some of it is just angry," which is a particularly evocative description of this track. Like some other songs on this soundtrack, "Tanhayee" is not lip-synced by the actors and there are lots of shots of Akash alone in reflective poses as he wanders locations in Sydney that he associates with Shalini.

In many ways, "Tanhayee" is closest in sound to a classic 1990s A. R. Rahman composition, in large part because of the emphasis on Indian classical flute sound, prominent use of drone, and the timbre of Sonu Nigam's voice. The song opens with a drone synth, haunting flute flourishes, and long delay in the background (this portion of the song is not included in the film itself). The bass line then anchors the beat and drives it forward. Programmed by Loy, the bass line has a phat, chunky analog sound to it that lends itself well to the "angry sad" emotion that the song conveys. The song is in a four-beat meter, but the phrasing and subdivision of the bass line makes it sound like it might be in an odd meter, almost like a seven beat meter (I had to listen to this many times carefully to confirm). This off-kilter approach to the bass is amplified by a drum accent on the offbeat of beat four that gives the song an unsettling feeling.

The vocal melody of the song builds in long phrases that include a large leap in the interval of the melodic hook, and Indian classical ornamentation/melisma (*gamaka*) that are matched by the flute. Indeed, one might argue that this moment foreshadows the sad flute line of "Kal Ho Na Ho" (2003) that signals the impending loss of the main character. The digital delay added to the voice singing "Tanhayee" (loneliness) keeps the notes resonating for seconds in the mix, amplifying the sense of aloneness, as though the singer were in a large, empty space. The lyrics ratchet up the tension, as Javed Akhtar deploys (perhaps somewhat overblown) poetic imagery of overwhelming youthful loss, a loss that seems like it will last forever.

This is a life that is now filled with despair (*mayusi*), broken dreams (*tute khwab*), a deepening darkness (*andheron ki ho gehrayi*), and general sense of hopelessness. Each of these lyrics is sung in a rising scale, that ends in a melodic cadence that suggests further confirmation of loss. Sonu conveys this sentiment quite effectively. The upper register of his voice has a haunting vulnerability to it that is quite beautiful: if Loy's bass line conveys the anger, Sonu's voice conveys the sadness. It is important to note that Sonu is perhaps best known for the songs that he recorded in the 2000s (e.g. *Kal Ho Na Ho* 2003), but his voice was one of ARR's regulars in his early period (e.g., *Dil Se* 1998) and he is one of the important post-Kishore Kumar and Mohammed Rafi male vocal prototypes of the 21st century.

The vocal and flute melodies have an appearance of being based upon a raga, albeit with some variation. The song ends with the lyric "Tanhayee" repeated in the singer's lower register, the final note on the dissonant second scale degree that slowly fades into the root. A very dark ending indeed. In a number of ways, the accompaniment to this song is quite spare—there is an openness to it that allows the use of digital effects to shine through. For instance, in the *antara*/verses, there is a call and response section between the singer and a barebones rhythm section (synth groove and rim shots on a ride cymbal). As a product of the recording studio, there are several places in which Naveen's flute has been stacked through multitrack recording, where he is playing a melody in octaves. As the go-to flautist in the industry, Naveen's sound is recognizable across film songs of the 1990s and beyond, including the ARR soundtracks to *Roja* (1992), *Bombay* (1995), *Dil Se* (1998), *Taal* (1999), as well as the soundtracks of many other music directors. He plays a large variety of flutes in both Indian classical and Western styles and in some ways is the most recognizable voice in film song that no one knows.

Track 8—Dil Chahta Hai (Reprise)

In many ways, the Reprise exemplifies the rock band aesthetic even more than the original version of the title track, as it has a more acoustic sound to it. The song plays during the end credits, a little more than three hours into the film, as the boys return to the iconic Chapora Fort location, then continues as the camera circles around the actors at a dinner party montage. The song uses the same lyrics and Shankar's vocal delivery is about the same. The tempo is a bit slower than the title track, with additional space provided by the sparse, offbeat bass line and hand percussion that pans between the channels. A Latin, quasi-montuno rhythm trades between the guitar and piano. This riff is coupled with the percussion, adding some variety to this version, as does arpeggiated guitar in a softer style than the first version. Piano is more prominent in this version, and Loy produces a nice jazz-style solo over a short vamp. Taken as a whole, the Reprise provides a good sense of the flexibility of the song, and of the musicians who perform it. It is also the version of "Dil Chahta Hai" that SEL plays in live performances, as this version allows for more musical flexibility.

4 *Dil Chahta Hai*'s Reception and Influence

As I pointed out in the Preface, it is not easy to separate the reception of an Indian soundtrack from the reception of its film—they are inextricably connected to each other. Much like standalone music videos, the meanings that one might draw from particular songs arrive packaged with preexisting narratives that are not readily dissociated from the film's narrative or the actors who are performing them in any particular scene. Only rarely do we see the actual musicians and vocalists performing the songs on screen, though there are some notable SEL examples like "Rind Posh Maal" from *Mission Kashmir* and Farhan Akhtar, Hritik Roshan, and Abhay Deol's actor-singer performance of "Senorita" in *Zindagi Na Milegi Dobara*. As media theorist Andrew Goodwin (1992) has warned, however, we must not take this idea of predetermined visual meanings too far: listeners very frequently bring their own durable interpretations of songs and lyrics in spite of the presence of a video track. As such, music becomes embodied in memory, which is absolutely the case in *Dil Chahta Hai* as the soundtrack of India's Millennial generation.

In their initial reviews of the film, critics noted that the film was oriented toward a cosmopolitan elite who had cut their teeth on English language films (it is noteworthy that Farhan Akhtar's original script was indeed written in English). There was a critical consensus that the film and its soundtrack were too "American" for the Indian masses and simply would not resonate. Although it was by no means a blockbuster at the box office, *DCH* did have a strong showing among urban youth in Mumbai and Delhi, which allowed it to at least break even. The cultural influence, however, was much greater than box office numbers might indicate. The film clearly resonated with what Ritty Lukose (2009) calls "Liberalization's children," a play on Salman Rushdie's *Midnight's Children* of Indian Independence. It is not difficult to find YouTube and commentary on this film about the impact that it had as a Millennial generational film in terms of the "natural" character dialogue, the fresh representations of friendship, the situational tensions, the confluence of Hindi and English languages, and so forth. As cultural critics have argued, this style of representing the wealthy urban youth became the approach *du jour* for many subsequent film directors and *DCH*'s defined one of the principal trajectories of Indian cinema of the 2000s. Many of these *DCH*-influenced films went on to grace the screens of emergent multiplexes: films made for an audience that could afford the escalating ticket prices. In other words, *DCH* is a kind of film that would become ubiquitous in the 2010s, a niche film with numerous economic risks that would only become commercially viable in the multiplex era.

The "naturalism" of the film is also derived from the sound design of the film. Along with *Lagaan*, *DCH* is one of the early uses of synchronized sound, as opposed to the still prevalent practice of dubbing the actor's voice in the studio after filming. Among other things, this adds a sense of the "room tone," or character of the myriad sounds in the background (AC hum, reverberations of the room, other ambient sounds) that created unique sound signatures for each of the locations and made the interactions seem more realistic as the actors worked in space (Chattopadhyay 2021). This makes for an acoustic presence to the film that is distinct from other films of the time, not the least of which is in the different timbres of actors' voices in a "natural" space as opposed to the performative context of an ADR studio in reenacting what the actor is seeing on screen (see Ganti 2012, 227–9 for a discussion of sound in Hindi cinema).

Beyond its cultural impact, DCH won many awards in both the "artistic" and "technical" categories. The technical category, I might add, frustrates many people involved in film production as it is usually an afterthought of audiences and does not get its own broadcast award show. The Filmfare Awards is often compared to the Oscars (Academy Awards), but would probably include the Grammys as well, since there were not yet national awards for albums in India at the time. The National Film Awards feature films in each of the regional language cinemas and tend to come from critic's perspective rather than simply gauging the relative popularity of a film. In broader terms, *Kabhi Khushi Kabhi Gham*, *Lagaan*, and *Dil Chahta Hai* were the three most nominated films of the year, with *Dil Chahta Hai* nominated in most of the artistic categories. In the 2002 award shows, the *Dil Chahta Hai* soundtrack came away with a number of honors, including Filmfare's RD Burman Award for New Music Talent, Screen magazine's awards for best music director and lyricist, and Udit Narayan's National Film Award as best playback singer for "Jaane Kyon." *Lagaan* came away with the most awards, including a nomination for the Best Foreign Language Film Oscar, the first film since *Salaam Bombay!* (1989) to be nominated. In terms of Indian music, only three Indian language films have been nominated for an Oscar, with two wins: *Slumdog Millionaire* (2009) and *RRR* (2023). In short, there was stiff competition that year. The International Indian Film Academy, a relatively new award ceremony at the time, similarly featured *DCH* in most of its musical categories. It is noteworthy that singers Alka Yagnik and Udit Narayan, and lyricist Javed Akhtar all won awards for their work on *Lagaan* in the same year.

In spite of the acclaim the soundtrack would later receive, the initial reviews of the music were largely lackluster, however. Critics celebrated the "freshness" of the soundtrack and its departure from the conventions of commercial Indian cinema. They tended to applaud "Woh Ladki" and "Jaane Kyon," the most conventional of the songs on the soundtrack. There was also an acknowledgment of the approach of the youth anthem "Koi Kahe" as an extension of Ehsaan and Loy's work in their band Instant Karma. Beyond that, however, critics of the time did not foresee the broad influence that the soundtrack would come to have in later Bollywood productions. Indeed, as I have argued, the success of *Dil Chahta Hai* helped create the conditions of possibility for the success of the rock band aesthetic that would be used by many other rock musician-cum-Indian music directors that would follow, such as Salim-Sulieman, Amit Trivedi, Pritam, and Vishal-Shekhar. Not only did it affect the ways that music directors approached composition and recording, but as Vijay Benegal notes in his interview later in the book, "[T]he sound of the album made people sit up and listen. I'm talking about engineers and musicians as well, because this was a very fresh new approach." It became a watershed album for the production of a new sound, one that emerged in the confluence of composer, musician, and studio producer, a mediation of Indian and Western musical conventions that emerged as another set of song possibilities. The result was something entirely new, a sound that was distinct from the mainstream of the time, a sound that heralded one of the futures of Indian cinematic musics.

More than anything else, as the interviews in the following chapters will indicate, *Dil Chahta Hai* changed the lives of everyone who was involved with it. The songs remain popular, audiences still sing along in live performances, and the album remains evergreen in Indian popular culture. To paraphrase Ehsaan, *Dil Chahta Hai* helped make Bollywood *cool*.

PART II

Interviews

As I mentioned at the beginning of the book, I did not anticipate that I would have the opportunity to interview the people involved in producing this album. Shankar, Ehsaan, Loy, and Farhan have any number of videos on YouTube and other streaming sites that were a fascinating font of information and provided me with many details about this soundtrack and how it intersected with their later work. Having this archive as a component of my research on *Dil Chahta Hai* enabled me to fine-tune my interviews with the producers and address some questions that were not available elsewhere, particularly more detailed questions about their approach as musicians and as composers from the perspective of another musician/musicologist who shares some of the musical language. Many of their insights into the broader production of Indian film song did not directly apply to any particular song on this soundtrack, but are noteworthy in and of themselves and may be intrinsically interesting to many readers. As a result, I have included the following chapters as a selection of the interviews with each of the composers and producers in order to give them their own voice. Each of these interviews took place via Zoom in late 2023 and were transcribed and edited to make them more readable.

5   Interview—Ehsaan Noorani (Composer, Musician)

October 27, 2023, Zoom

Jayson Beaster-Jones
Twenty to twenty-three years from *Dil Chahta Hai*, what do you remember about the process?

Ehsaan Noorani
The thing is, Farhan Akhtar approached us, we hadn't really got into composing for films, then we had done a couple of films. One film never got made called *Dus* which meant "ten," and another film which we did a couple of songs. Farhan approached us saying that he was making this film, and kind of briefed us in a way. It was very different at the script stage, even when we heard it—not like the regular Hindi films that we watch. So he gave us a brief about the music and also said, "That's my first movie, so if you guys don't come up with anything, give me the option that, you know, I can work with someone else." And we said "sure, of course." Then we went out of town to hill station near Bombay. Ritesh, he had a lovely house there up in the hills. We set up together and went there to compose music, and we went for about ten days, saying that's how long it's going to take us. Like Led Zeppelin went into the country to compose. [laughs] Anyway, so we landed

up composing all the songs in two days, with lyrics in the third day with all the songs ready, with the structure and with the content of the songs ready.

JBJ

Have there been other soundtracks that you all composed that came together that quickly?

Ehsaan

In the same way? Well, actually, we did do a couple of soundtracks that we went out of town for a couple of movies and it wasn't as successful. We did a film called *Kal Ho Na Ho*, which was actually one of our biggest films. We went out of town, and we were there for three days, but we came back with only one song. That happens. So we did it for a couple of movies, and then after that, I think with the work pressure, the time factor, we didn't really get to do it that much.

JBJ

Did you take this sort of jam band style of writing? Did people come in with ideas that they wanted to try out?

Ehsaan

Well actually, the thing is that while we were driving up to Lonavala, actually, it's a very rainy day, I remember, when I told Benny [Vijay Benegal] "you drive" because you know, he's a much better driver than I am. So he said, "Okay, I'll drive" and then we listened to an album on the way up called the *Afro Celt Sound System*. They did three or four albums for the Real World label and very good stuff. It's all mixed: a mixture of Africa, world music—and let's say in the early 2000s, in fact, 1990s to the early 2000s world music was very big in terms of what Peter Gabriel did and movies like *Last Temptation of Christ* and stuff. So, we will listen to this album and as soon as we reached Khandala, and we set up, Shankar said, "let's do it. Let's do it, like a Celtic kind song, a River Dance kind of thing." And he started playing this line [sings pipe melody to "Woh Ladki"], that line. We composed the song around that, where it was just beautiful.

JBJ
I've seen reference to that soundtrack a few times now, I had suspected that "Woh Ladki" emerged from that experience, but thanks for confirming that that's how it made it in.

Ehsaan
That album was very strong when you heard it so that's a lovely sound which has never been heard in Hindi film industry, so we said, "let's bring that sound in."

JBJ
Do you remember what at all the instructions you were given about, like where the song situations were going to be?

Ehsaan
No, but actually, what we did do is before we went out of town, we had a little jam in a friend's back room, it was a recording studio. We didn't want to hire the studio. So in the back room, we came up with the main riff, which is for "Dil Chahta Hai," which is [sings "Dil Chahta Hai" bass line] and actually that was for a different song situation in the film, a song called "Jaane Kyon." So Farhan said, let's hang on to this bass line and then maybe use it in that song. We were in Khandala, I remember very clearly Shankar was brushing his teeth, came out of the

bathroom saying that "Man, we can use our bass line for the title song," [sings] "Dil Chahta Hai". Then suddenly—like even we hadn't eaten breakfast—we just got into the groove and we completed that idea, just got that song locked in.

JBJ
So I'm just thinking about process and how you guys approach songwriting generally: someone came with an idea, and you sort of jammed around that to figure out what's going to work?

Ehsaan
Right. In fact, the thing is that the way we work is literally the three of us. When we're in the studio—I mean, not in this situation where we were out of town, because we didn't have enough equipment then and whatnot—but we go to the studio, we have your central computer, which is running ProTools, or whatever like that, and we still work in a very archaic way where we send MIDI timecode MPC to all three of us. So all of us are locked onto the computer. We get a song idea, we go for a common tempo which we entered into a computer, saying that we were working this tempo. Then maybe I'll track four bars of guitar, Shankar will put down a little line. Now we'll put in a comp or a groove. So everything's getting recorded on the computer, it's all getting into ProTools. Then what we do is we listen to the ideas that we put down and then edit them together. Then you see that you've got a song kind of thing happening. Like, "let's not use this B part from here, let's use the B part for some other part." So that's the process—it's a very organic process in the sense that it's nothing that's preconceived, or you know, we're going to do this style of music—except if the brief asked for it. Like we did

a film called *Rock On*—that is like that was probably the first rock soundtrack in India, because it's about a rock band. We literally did that the way a band would compose—so we got the drummer and a friend of ours to play bass. We went to the studio, I was plugged in, and we composed the songs like a band. The drummer, Darshan, says, "I'll play a groove like this." Essentially just like a band, an organic sound like a garage band.

JBJ
So you would make the argument that *Rock On* would be the first rock album rather than *Dil Chahta Hai*?

Ehsaan
I would say that *Dil Chahta Hai* was the first film soundtrack to bring in rock elements like the guitar solo or the title song, and that kind of stuff which was never done before. For the first time we use trance in a song, "Koi Kahe," the dance song; the whole world music influence in "Jaane Kyon" where we added the didgeridoo and stuff like that from Australia. It was a true eclectic sounding album. We were not pressured in any way to live up to anything that we've done, not necessarily be influenced by all the Indian elements and the kind of music that's gone down in the years past. Yes, we were definitely listening to a lot of A. R. Rahman because I mean, he's pretty good, and so maybe that is a bit of—not an influence, but a bit of charge for us. But the rest of it we just did with the current music that we listen to, and the kind of music we found. That's what Farhan listens to as well.

JBJ
That sounds like it was a fairly critical dimension: if Farhan was into an older style of Bollywood, then that would have been a very different kind of soundtrack.

Ehsaan

It would have been very different. Yeah, very different.

JBJ

You must have negotiated with each other about what each song would be, or what situation it was going to fill?

Ehsaan

Actually not much, because it was just one of those projects that was kind of magical—everything that we focused on would literally fall into place. The thing is, the director, Farhan, is very open in his briefs, and he likes you to compose in terms of that—it's not like that he takes on any commercial pressure, that "I want a song like this" and "it should be that way." It's just like, "let's see what we come up with. And if you don't like it, we'll come back tomorrow and do something else."

JBJ

And when you're presenting songs to him, you are presenting rough tracks of what you've recorded?

Ehsaan

Absolutely, rough tracks. Because the thing is when you focus, you've got a good melody, that is your first part of the song. That is key. And then everything that you dress around it, you can present a song in any way. Like I said, it depends on the script, like *Rock On* was all rock and that's the way we presented the music. The thing is, he's there with us all the time through the composition process. He's never not there.

JBJ

That seems fairly unusual.

Ehsaan
Not really, because it is his movie. He is the captain of the ship and we like his input, with him, Zoya [Akhtar], all of them actually. They like to be there when you're creating the song. The thing was that he's very musically tuned in, to see what is good, what is bad. It's not like "Oh, man, I'm not sure." There's no "I'm not sure." There's no gray area. "Yes or no." And that is a good thing. When you work with the director like that, it lets your creativity flow.

JBJ
I can appreciate that. The more someone dithers, the harder it becomes to compose something.

Ehsaan
Absolutely, absolutely.

JBJ
I talked with Benny [Vijay Benegal] earlier and he said that he was introduced to the mukhda-antara form through this album and that he needed to ask about what it was. How were you guys thinking about song forms at the time?

Ehsaan
What actually, the thing is that we decided that we'd go with the traditional song form because of Javed Akhtar; we had just started working with him. He was also from a trad background, but his words were as modern as they could be for the songs. So we decided we'd go for the mukhda-antara kind of thing because that's what people are used to. We said, "Let's not shock people."

JBJ

As I listened to the song forms, it sounds like you're playing with things a little bit. I'm hearing a bridge here and there, I'm hearing what sounds like a proto verse-chorus kind of form, but sutured on to a mukhda-antara lyrical structure.

Ehsaan

Yeah, that's true. The thing is, in the melodic form, you bring the hook back at the end of the *antara*, which is how it was. With Hindi songs, though, they start with the chorus first and then get into the verse. The point is you want to hook people from the beginning. And it's a very interesting way of writing. I'm pretty sure that it would probably work in Western music as well, you get the hook at the beginning, not wait for the hook to come. I thought that it's a pretty interesting way of working. But now with new people that we work with, the new films that we work with, they prefer also go for verses and a bridge the way it is in Western music. The thing is also that the attention span of people has become shorter because of streaming and stuff like that. So you don't want a very long song.

JBJ

So where a typical song would have been like 6 or 7 minutes, you're now down to 4 minutes? I hadn't noticed that, because the idea is you're trying to catch them before they move on to the next stream?

Ehsaan

Yes.

JBJ

A guitarist colleague of mine loved your approach to the guitar solo in "Dil Chahta Hai." He praised your restraint, because you lay the idea out there and give a little space, and then lay the next idea out there and give a little space. My colleague said, "Yeah, I would have been all over that. I would just play all the way through."

Ehsaan
[laughs] So that's the thing that I've always done, because I'm coming from a strong background doing commercials and jingles for many years—I may have composed probably 1000 jingles by now. You always worked with creating something that was memorable. So the thing is that the albums you hear—maybe not on *Rock On*, but even on *Rock On*—you hear that my guitar solos are very quotable. It becomes a part of the song. It's a cool thing to do, because you're also not given such a long space solo over. It's not like you're Deep Purple or something does that. [laughs]

JBJ
No 15-minute guitar solos?

Ehsaan
Yeah, absolutely. Actually with "Dil Chahta Hai" it's very interesting. That solo which I played, I literally just did a jam. I just played what came off the top of my head. Then I wanted to change it, and these guys—Benny, Loy, Shankar, Farhan—did not let me change the solo! If you hear the solo on headphones, there's a wrong note that is like a harmonic, the ring tone. I wanted to change that—they wouldn't let me change that. They said, "No way, man. We like it this way!" But that's a wrong note!

JBJ
Now I'm going to go back and listen for it.

Ehsaan

You hear a "ping," like a hydro trigger.

JBJ

Do you play the same solo or do you adjust when playing this live?

Ehsaan

The version that we do live nowadays is the Reprise, and maybe it's longer. We have a sax player and I play a much longer solo. The solo that I play is kind of, yes, rocky. Yeah it's bluesy, but I do a lot of outside jazz kind of stuff with that as well.

JBJ

I imagine "Dil Chahta Hai," the song, you must have performed live hundreds of times by now.

Ehsaan

Absolutely every gig. We can't leave that out.

JBJ

So it's become one of the defining songs, like if you go to see Prince, you're not going to leave until you heard "Purple Rain"?

Ehsaan

Of course.

JBJ

So you have a set of songs you perform live, a hit from here hit from here hit from there?

Ehsaan

Yeah, you can't not do some songs. It's like you said, you can't expect the Rolling Stones not to do "Satisfaction." The thing is that we've had forty number one songs, so there's so many songs that we still can perform, we need to rework the set, but sometimes that's risky. So you work for what kind of gig that you do. If you do a public gig, then you can pull in other songs. If you're doing a marriage gig, then you do some other songs there. If you make a corporate gig, that is something else. It all depends on that.

JBJ

This means then that your catalog of possible songs has grown over the last twenty to twenty-five years. How often are you guys playing live these days?

Ehsaan

Well actually, we just played live like a few days ago in Calcutta, now we're going to Rajasthan in four days' time for a corporate gig. Shankar does his own gigs as well. It's a fairly good pace.

JBJ

Also, the number of YouTube videos you do, talking about guitar riffs and those sorts of things.

Ehsaan

Yeah, yeah. That's my favorite.

JBJ

Thank you for doing that, because it makes my job easier to figure out where you all are coming from! Thinking along that line, this is in the back of my mind, how did you transition to becoming a celebrity?

Ehsaan

Well, actually, I'll tell you something, Jayson, nothing was planned for. I mean, I really didn't ever think that I'd be composing music for Bollywood. The thing is, I listened to a lot of Hindi film music growing up, because my mom had the radio on all the time, and that was good. I watched a lot of Hindi films when I was a kid, like many of them. But the thing is that once I got into rock and roll and everything else that went with it, I started slowly moving away from that kind of stuff, especially in the 1990s, where I think the film industry kind of took a dip, where it was really poorly made films and some not so good music coming out. I wouldn't say it was bad, but I say it was not good. At that time I had no intention of getting into the film industry. I mean, I'm gonna be happy doing jingles and making good money. We were at the pinnacle in terms of that genre of commercial music. We were playing in a blues band, we were doing that kind of thing as well. Mukul Anand approached me to do the music for this film called *Dus*. Initially, I kind of didn't want to do it because I didn't want to get into the film thing then. He was a regular client of mine doing advertising. So he said, "You have to do it." So I said, "Okay, I want to just work with these two guys." And the rest is history, literally, like it was fated to happen.

JBJ

So how did you know Loy and Shankar? Had you worked with them on other projects?

Ehsaan

Loy used to live in Delhi and used to do commercial work, then he moved down to Bombay. Even now we are really good friends, we get along very well, musically, philosophically, every way. And so the thing is that we did a lot of work together. And Shankar was still working with Oracle at that time. Like a good South Indian, he was part of the computer and the IT thing, and he was going to go to America. He got a job already in Silicon Valley and he just made this decision at the last minute that "I want to do music." So he was around. We used to use him for jingles, and he'd come and arrange things with us. So that was it: we decided that we'd work together on one project which never happened. That was really disappointing, because we said, "You know, man, maybe this is what it's supposed to be. It's not supposed to happen." Then one project happened, then the second project happened, and then *Dil Chahta Hai* happened and everything changed.

JBJ

I know you're tied to the fortunes of the film in certain kinds of ways, but I'm curious, did *Dil Chahta Hai* become a way that you all approached soundtracks in the future?

Ehsaan

Well actually what happened was initially, a lot of the projects we did they said, "It's not sounding like *Dil Chahta Hai*." There are some other people who say it's too much like *Dil Chahta Hai*. It is not true. I mean, it was never like that. It was just the way people perceive things. Now you've got these music supervisors who work with different designs. Any music composer goes over the song which has guitar and drums, and they say, "No, that sounds like Shankar-Ehsaan-Loy," which is kind of silly because all our songs are not like that—we do all kinds of styles. But yes, people are looking for a different sound, to show a different approach to songwriting, and different production, which came out in all the work that we did. That this was well-produced, it was lush sounding, it was different. You couldn't put a finger on that, no two albums sounded the same. There's no repetition melodically or of the idea itself in terms of the concept. You have all the different albums, *Bunti aur Babli*, *Kal Ho Na Ho*, *Rock On*, *Don*, *Zindagi Na Milegi*, all are different.

JBJ
Yeah, this is something I appreciate because I can see that you all are still continuing to explore the musical universe. Usually there's a couple of songs on every soundtrack where I think, "Okay, I get a sense that they were listening to flamenco at that time," or something like that.

Ehsaan
Yeah, absolutely.

JBJ
This is a very deliberate choice on your part, that you're trying new things. You must have conversations about this: "Well, we did this in our previous soundtrack, so let's move in a different direction?"

Ehsaan
Absolutely. The thing is, most of that comes from me, because I tend to be very objective, super objective to the point where I've had fights with them. I've left the band about twenty times. [laughs] Basically, it is important to maintain a certain freshness in every project. So we kind of mold ourselves to the script of the film. Luckily, with Loy, me, and Shankar with his entire knowledge of folk and classical and philosophy coming from rock and blues. This is jazz, playing classical, there's a lot that we

can do. The experience of doing commercials has exposed me to many different kinds of music, whether it's African or others. We've done films with all kinds of settings, so that taught me a lot. We are able to add those influences into our music if needed, like if they want the song to have a Chinese feel to that.

JBJ
So this means that you're constantly listening. Thinking around the year 2000, you mentioned the Afro-Celtic album, were there other things you were listening to at the time?

Ehsaan
Listening to a lot of producer William Orbit. A lot of Madonna "Ray of Light," soundtrack to *The Beach*, Leonardo DiCaprio. A lot of synthesizer and trancie kind of things. But at the same time, I was listening to a lot of Robin Ford and Larry Carlton and BB King who just kept going on. I was listening to a lot of jazz funk, what they called acid jazz. So there was that happening. So listening to a lot of stuff like William Orbit was a big influence. You can hear it in a couple of our soundtracks like *Don*. You get synthesizers, and that kind of thing.

JBJ
Within *Dil Chahta Hai* is there any particular moment that you're thinking, say, "this is from somewhere else"? Meaning this particular sound, or this particular solo, that sort of thing? Like this is my Robin Ford moment?

Ehsaan
Not really. I mean there are times. There's a scene, which the guys are playing volleyball on the beach ["Rockin' Goa"]. We thought

like, "Let's do this song like 'Mysterious Ways' by U2." Now when you hear it, it doesn't sound anything like "Mysterious Ways," but if you connect the two after I've told you, it's like you put the two pieces together. Tempo is exactly the same, because Farhan cut the film to the music around that.

JBJ

When you were in the recording studio, what gear were you using when you recorded?

Ehsaan

Actually for *Dil Chahta Hai*, besides playing guitar, I do a lot of synthesizer stuff as well. Little grooves. I'm really into synthesizers. I love synthesizers. I've always loved them. So I like textures, and that kind of production, adding stuff in. So there's a whole bunch of synths that I had then. Now, of course, one laptop suffices. I had a lot of hardware since I had a rack, which is about six feet high. Guitar wise, my setup is very simple: I used my black Paul Reed Smith, which I bought in 1986 when I was in the United States. That's what I use for most, actually all, of the songs. The Yamaha acoustic guitar, which is what I play.

JBJ

Do you prefer electric over acoustic?

Ehsaan

I love acoustic but I'm not very good at playing acoustic, because I find it very tough. My fingers are very small. Electric, I just love electric.

JBJ

Did you have any pedals that you were using, that you remember?

Ehsaan

All the guitar solos and everything from *Dil Chahta Hai*, I had this Tech 21 Sansamp pedal, which was like an analog amp simulator, which actually sounded very good. That's what I used for most of the soundtrack. The rest of the effects and stuff came from ProTools.

JBJ

Thinking back to *Dil Chahta Hai*, what's your favorite song?

Ehsaan

Oh, that's a tough one. Every time I hear the album, a different song. But my one favorite song, and that would be "Kaisi Hai Yeh Rut." I love all the textures. The other day Loy and I were trying to work out what I played, because I double tracked all the guitars. And I couldn't figure out, like, "You know, man, what do we do here?" [laughs] We listened back to that. We love that soundtrack.

JBJ

And so you were playing acoustic on that. It sounds like you had a chorus pedal?

Ehsaan

That's electric.

JBJ

That was electric!?

Ehsaan

Yeah, I used to have a single coil kind of split sound, which gave it an acoustic-y feel, but it was not acoustic. All of it is double tracked. So the inversions that we have played, like different inversions. So in fact, a lot of players who try to transcribe that song couldn't figure out what I played [laughs]. In fact, we did some pretty crazy things on the album. There's a song on that album called "Jaane Kyon." In the antara of the song, or whatever you want to call it, because that's always got a different format—it's not the typical *mukhda-antara*—there were these chords that Loy wrote. So what we did was we actually use six tracks, and tracked each note of the chord on a separate track, so that we can get the spread.

JBJ

Thinking about the background vocals, when I was listening with musician friends, we were comparing it to Men at Work or Steely Dan in terms of that kind of aesthetic.

Ehsaan

That is really where we were coming from.

JBJ

If you were writing this book, is there anything that you would want people to know about the soundtrack, how it's changed your life, or anything along that line?

Ehsaan

An interesting thing was that a lot of musicians met us, not only musicians, all kinds of people told us that "we never listened to Bollywood music earlier, but now *Dil Chahta Hai* has made Bollywood music cool." A lot of musicians who are rock musicians told us, "You gave us hope that producing an album that is popular is possible for us." Indian musicians do, and that's really what's happening now, Amazon and stuff, people are doing that kind of stuff. So we've been a catalyst to start a kind of movement. This is a historical album, it was at one stage in every record shop, when you could get CDs and stuff, that it would be in the top 20 charts. Then in 2022–23 *Dil Chahta Hai*, years after, it was a catalog item.

JBJ
If you were to distinguish yourself in the music you were creating from what Rahman was doing at the time, how would you distinguish your approach from his?

Ehsaan
I think the thing is, I think our music is very, very eclectic. It doesn't have a particular stamp on it, where you could recognize it as–I mean, yeah, you could recognize it as our music—but you can't say that, "This is typically of them." I don't think that we've had anything that has released that's been typically of us. I mean, rock is something that you use. But then, when a blues guitar player does a blues album, you don't see that's typically of them. So if there's overdriven guitar and there's riffs and stuff, yes, that is rock, but that doesn't mean that it's the same as *Rock On*, is the same as *Dil Chahta Hai*. If you use it as an influence.

JBJ
Despite this eclecticism, the different kinds of styles that you're using, you have a different kind of recognizable sound.

Ehsaan
I think 80 percent of that is just the songwriting that you write melodically to make sure that it's a good album. And you hear a new album which came out? Unfortunately, the movie didn't do well, called *Dono*. That's on iTunes and Amazon, it

is not on Spotify. You can check that soundtrack out. It's very wholesome, melodic. Very ethnic, yet modern. There's a lot of good stuff on that. Unfortunately, we have no control about how a movie does. So if the movie goes, the soundtrack goes with it most of the time.

6 Interview—Loy Mendonsa (Composer, Musician)

October 31, 2023, Zoom

Jayson Beaster-Jones
What do you remember back in the heady days of 2000–01?

Loy Mendonsa
I think, firstly, just a little bit of premise of generally Bollywood's 'scape. It's had its movement and its influences by whatever's popular at the time. You can hear it—the various musicians that have come in, arrangers, and the whole lot. So, it's a logical journey up to that point. I think all three of us bring our influences into the music, all the stuff that we grew up with. Shankar comes with his Indian classical stuff; Ehsaan with his blues and rock; and I come from a bit of [Western] classical and a lot of jazz—I got into jazz at one point very heavily. Those are my main influences, and cinema overall and a lot of world music. My dad would have all these albums of Mongo Santa Maria. He came home with albums—it was not like LPs, but they were long playing, but they were a little smaller. You bought them in boxes. Everyday after school, I would come in, drop the needle on one, and then kind of figure out, "Oh, man, this is a different universe," jump to the next. So all that is sunk in very subconsciously.

So when we came in we were passionate about our influences and there was no way of directly putting it into anything apart from the ads that we do. We do a lot of jingles. Most of the bands that we would play in would be like a cover band doing blues and rock stuff like that. So when this project came on, especially this film, I don't think we even realized that they wanted a "young" sound because no one really said it. No one really articulated that "we need to have something modern and young." It was just the crew was selected and everything fell in place. I think there was lots of stuff within us that needed to get out. We heard the script and said, "Hey, this is very cool." The other thing is that we did not have a face: SEL did not have a face. There wasn't even a name to start with, so it was a blank canvas and we could set the course the way we wanted to. That's a great thing, because there's no pressure.

JBJ
So basically the whole world is open.

Loy
Yes, yes. We could navigate to any point that we wanted to, and I think it's an evolution … it evolved very beautifully. The whole process was extremely organic. The process was basically writing the melodies first, and then, a lot of times while the melody was happening, we would write the harmonic stuff, the riffs, and lines. It's almost like a band jamming. It's the same concept when you're writing an arrangement: you'll do sketches of various parts, like a riff section, maybe just a fluid section. Then as you step back, it starts coming together, you say, "Oh wait, this would be better here, and this will be better here," that kind of thing. One day you all have it all in your head in its totality.

JBJ

Do you have a sense of what each person tended to contribute to the overall sound? Or was there a lot of mixture between the three of you?

Loy

There was a lot of mixture, but I think Ehsaan and Shankar wrote a lot more on that one. I was looking at it from just the sonics and the treatment of the changes, the harmonies, stuff like that–bass lines, all that. Some parts I would tweak the melody if I had to modulate it. I'd say "Okay, try this." and stuff. So it was–and it still is–the same method that we followed from then to now. It's very organic. Anyone can come at any point and say, "Hey, this is a possibility." We preview it. So that was the process. [pause] We got some beautiful melodies that evolved. We were initially supposed to write for, I think, five days or a week. And we pretty much wrote all of it in three days. It just fell in place.

JBJ

Thanks for giving me a sense of your background. The world music influence makes a lot of stuff click into place for me, I've heard like montunoes and various kinds of applications of montunoes coming in your playing. In *Mission Kashmir*, for example, I was hearing a reggae sound making its way in. In this soundtrack, obviously, there's "Jaane Kyon" and the African inspired sound. There's also the Irish inspired-sound in "Woh Ladki."

Loy

Yeah, it's all there. Like I said with the influences—also the Irish thing if you want to look at it—is because we've heard bagpipes in the Army bands. Subconsciously it's all there. I mean, people have heard it, it's not alien, you know what I mean? But it's not mainstream. It's not like a fiddle that someone's playing or banjo or whatever. It's like second layer, third layer, if you want to call it that. It's like tubas in marching bands. It's not what folk musicians play, but people have heard it. People have heard that sound.

JBJ
That's interesting, because then you're only really one degree of remove, maybe two degrees of remove, from something that's a familiar sound.

Loy
They've heard it, perhaps audiences have not paid too much attention to it. If you heard in the military music, or bands playing at the back, this becomes part of that whole thing; it becomes that event, and then people move out into their regular lives and it's forgotten.

JBJ
Do they continue to associate it with, say, military bands? Or, is there another association there?

Loy
I don't think they're even aware of it. I tend to analyze a lot of this stuff. For me it's very interesting to see where the where the junction is, so to speak

JBJ
If I remember correctly, you're coming out of Herbie Hancock musically, and 1960s–70s jazz?

Loy
A lot of jazz. As a matter of fact, I think a lot of Coltrane was there, and I can hear parts of it even. It's very subtle—a lot of stuff that I use, like certain ride cymbals where I wanted to get

that feeling of Bill Stewart, or one of those ECM [record label] drummers that play that floaty kind of sound. Not as aggressive as Tony Williams with so much ping, but it's much more airy, you know, very floaty. So all those are those things, they're my influences, I listen to that kind of stuff. I am very fond of that kind of music. I like the funk stuff. I just like good music.

JBJ
I don't actually know much of your biography coming into this project. I know you were in Delhi before you connected with Ehsaan and Shankar. You were composing jingles?

Loy
I was writing jingles, I was doing a lot of work for theater when I was in Delhi. We did a lot of music and I was writing for a lot of theater out there, and of course television when that happened. Then I moved back to Mumbai because I couldn't go beyond that. I said, "Nothing happening here." I wanted to be in the thick of it, so I came back home to Mumbai.

JBJ
You grew up in Mumbai?

Loy
I grew up in Mumbai and played in a couple of bands. Actually, my band got a contract to go to Delhi, so I went with them. We did it for a couple of years, and then I came back. I was writing a lot at that time. It's weird because I lost my job when my son was born—I literally had one month's money in the bank. [laughs] One month's rent, on the edge. So I said, "Hey, this is not a good place to be and I need to find something much more solid now that I'm a dad and family man." So I started writing jingles and commercials and doing stuff like that. Then

the plays came out of it and small stuff: theater, kids theater, and stuff like that.

JBJ
For the theater, was it largely background scoring or sound design?

Loy
Scores, some songs.

JBJ
Knowing that your musical influences are coming out of a complicated era within jazz, in *Dil Chahta Hai*, I think I've heard you sneak in some extended chords here and there [Loy laughs] a ninth here, an eleventh there. Have you ever had to rein yourself in?

Loy
No, not really, because a lot of people, especially the newer kids now, when they look at it, and they start, it becomes an exercise as to what chords you can throw in. I keep telling them that you can technically harmonize every note many ways that you want to, but when you're writing a song, the main thing is that I have to leave you with a certain feeling. We are always very sensitive to—if I play like a C minor or an F sus—what would be the difference? There are common notes to all. You will react differently to a C minor seven versus to an F sus. You know what I'm saying?

JBJ
I do. So that's something I've been wrestling with for a really long time: for people who know Western music, for that F sus,

it wants to go somewhere. [Yeah] That four, that eleven, it really needs to resolve somehow. But I've long been wondering whether Indian audiences, who aren't necessarily steeped in Western harmonic knowledge, are they necessarily going to hear that in the same way?

Loy
I would say from my experience—from both cultures, be it Indian and be it Western—I think that a lot of people who don't hear harmony the way it's supposed to be heard. There are some people who know–they can sense that there's something happening and they can't put their finger on it. You know, it's like that. You can sense there's something in the food—I don't know what it is, but it tastes great. There's something I don't even know, I'm not the chef. You just need to experience it, that's all.

JBJ
Yeah, that's a great analogy. So there's this spice in here, I can't quite place it but I know that it's making something else pop.

Loy
That's it, yeah.

JBJ
One of the things I've noticed in the way that you all record is that harmony is at the front and center of what you do. As opposed to a lot of other music directors up to, say, 1990 where harmony is pretty low in the mix. You can hear it if you're listening for it, but it's not right there. It strikes me that the way you all record, harmony is right at the center.

Loy

It's important as part of the canvas. There are certain tunes that you write that fall back into the drone, almost like a tanpura concept where they have fixed this I-V [cadence]. Like I said, Coltrane's band did the same thing, just [sings "da boom, boom, boom" from "Equinox"]. But conceptually, it's the same thing. Use a bigger drone using upright bass, it's like using a tanpura. If you pull out the instruments, you understand conceptually what's happening. It's almost the same thing. Coltrane was playing all this complex stuff, then of course, all the other stuff. Like I said, those are all our influences and bringing that into it, but being very cautious not to be in front. I don't want to be in front of the voice in front of the song, I need to be behind. I need to be that thing behind you.

How do I put it in perspective? [pause] It's not just the canvas, it is little more than the canvas. As opposed to someone coming in just painting on the canvas, but assume that the canvas is not white. It already had a kind of preset tone to it. A backup tone, whatever you want to call it, and that is also dictated by the melody. The melody had a certain thing, then we all bring our textures: Ehsaan brings certain layers of guitars, I would do some synths, depending on how much space there is, and requirement-wise. We always like to keep a lot of space in the music, because I think that's as important as other things.

JBJ

I'm thinking about the harmonic component as shifting: the canvas is shifting colors as you go, but you are trying to find things that remain complementary along with that. [Yeah] And so do you all tend to write melodically and then harmonize afterward?

Loy

Sometimes, but sometimes it's very fluid. While Shankar is singing, we are both playing, and we come up with these progressions. Ehsaan might come with a riff or a line—so that's a nice line and we can build up on it, and vice versa. So we'd find a part, add some textures on top of the chord progression, stuff like that. What tends to happen, especially if you come from classical music, you tend to always write from an Indian perspective as a raag, like a mode of songs. You write Lydian [mode] and that certain sound has a certain feeling. But then you get stuck in the Lydian and you can't get out of it. A lot of times we say, "Okay, we'll break that." Sometimes a starting point is the Lydian thing and we can move out if we need to. It's not tied in.

JBJ

You're thinking about this in sort of Western modal terms, rather than in terms of raga form or playing from a particular raag?

Loy

There are some songs or some tunes that might have a stronger raag thing to it. But a lot of the stuff that we did, sometimes we would move things out of [raga] and I didn't realize it, because unknowingly, or probably just intuitively, doing it. We met a couple of guys who play guitar, and they were coming from a classical background and they would come up and say, "But you started on this raag, and then you suddenly went to this." And I said, "Did we do that?" The analysis is coming from the other side. [laughs]

JBJ

Well there is that long history within Hindi cinema on some level drawing from raga. But I've never actually been convinced that people are truly drawing from a raag when they say, "This is, you know, borrowed from Raag Yaman," I suspect that they're thinking about it in terms of mode, rather than thinking about it in terms of raag, including the associated melodic patterns, and so forth.

Loy

It's a raag.

JBJ

Yeah, it is. But are they always referencing the melodies that go along with that raag?

Loy

The system is such that they've done so much. It's part of the tradition, that you just hear it from the time you're a kid. You're either hearing it on radio, or you're hearing it in religious ceremonies. There are certain *bhajans* and songs that have a certain sound. When I was growing up, I would hear a lot of stuff—like there was the Ganesha festival. I would hear the Yaman raag being played out there. And I didn't realize it till much later when I was trying to study modes and raags and I said "oh, It's the same thing."

JBJ

Thinking of "Tanhayee," there's this flat nine thing going in there: you didn't just say, "Hey, let's draw from this raag"?

Loy

No, because the trigger to the song was the bass line. I found this patch on my synth and I had this [sings "Tanhayee" bass line] and Shankar walked into the room with Javed Sahib and he heard this line and he said, "Hey, that's very interesting." And they started writing immediately on top of it. So that was the trigger, that was the process of writing. It could be a groove, it could be a chord progression. This one was the bass line of Tanhayee [sings it]. And then everything kind of was written around from that. We built on that.

JBJ
It's a great sound. I think that's one of the songs that you were slipping into some extended harmonies.

Loy
Yeah, those had some elevens and a minor six. I personally feel "Dil Chahta Hai," the title song, was interesting because it had a lot of not normal changes. It's more coming from R&B because of the C minor, A flat, and then goes to F sus—I'm just calling the chords, not in order. Then goes to B flat major seven, D minor, G minor—so it's got all those things, which is not really part of traditional Bollywood writing. Someone playing R&B—and there's more harmony among the jazz player—you just can hear it and play it on the first shot. For the harmonic R&B player, but not for a pop player. Maybe today's pop player, or the '90s guys, but not some of the players coming up. Like I said, I listened to anything that's good, harmony it's interesting.

JBJ
That makes it hard to then pin down at any given point if three sets of hands are touching a particular song or a synth line. [Right] You can't be like, "This is the characteristic SEL sound but not necessarily a characteristic Loy sound that's being used here."

Loy

Yeah. The "Dil Chahta Hai" groove was Shankar's idea [sings drum rhythm]. It's almost like an R&B adapted groove. It does that funk thing–James Brown kind of things are coming from that. It is very weird because Shankar hears stuff, a lot of times he's not familiar with it, he just kind of feels a certain thing, and he just plays it. [laughs] I think a lot of us tend to do that, just be in the moment, whatever your influences, whatever seeps into you. You're not saying, "hey, I want to do a lot of that or this," that's never the case.

JBJ

So it's not like, "the way that the drummer in Parliament Funkadelic approaches this?" [No no no] So you said that you and Ehsaan are really into synths, when did this start for you?

Loy

I started off playing guitar, I play a lot of rhythm guitar. Initially, a little bit of bass. But when I started playing keyboards, many years ago, I just said, "it's nice in terms of writing, because it's easier to move in different keys." Plus it is much more visual. I don't think my brain is wired for visualizing the guitar, it's like a mystery. Some people are so good at it, some aren't. But I think the keyboard is nice because you can see everything and get an overview of a lot of things. Synths also have a nice thing to it, the soundscapes that you can get from it are quite fantastic.

JBJ

It sounds like you also spend a lot of time sort of working through the patches [synthesized sounds] and what the patches can do.

Loy

Yeah, and I think Ehsaan also plays a key role because he's got a great memory for patches. In the old days when we used to work together doing jingles, he'll say, "Oh, is this patch number so and so?" So he knows exactly! [laughs] I would normally take a book and write down my favorite patches. His memory is great at phone numbers, and remembering things. I don't think any more because we're all kind of getting on as the years go by. [laughs]

JBJ

His superpower is being able to remember numbers. [Yeah.] Do you remember the name of the patch for the Tanhayee groove, that Moog kind of sound?

Loy

I think there were two synths. I think one was Roland. I think I stacked two of them. Was it the Korg Triton? I think that's what Shankar has—I think it was a Triton, if I'm not mistaken. One of the earlier synths. It could also be the Korg Z1—that's the one we used on "Koi Kahe" [sings arpeggiated synth line] The Korg Z1 with a filter on it. It could be that but it seems to have a lot of resonance [sings bass line to Tanhayee, emphasizing oscillating filter]. It's got that kind of thing happening on it.

JBJ

Yeah, it was just a big phat sound. [Yeah. Yeah.] It strikes me you threw in some modulations into a couple of songs as well.

Loy

On "Kaisi Hai Yeh Rut." Yeah, it was the second or third time. So "Dil Chahta Hai" was a problem because Ehsaan and me come from a Western perspective, we always see the key as like a C minor and Shankar sees it from an F perspective, because he writes it. It was written from an Indian raag perspective. It's different—so for us, like the C minor was the C minor seven sus. So he was seeing it as an F. Both of us viewed differently, and he used it to fit. [laughs]

JBJ
So like this, there are several musical languages that are coming together. [Yes.] It doesn't seem like it requires you to necessarily negotiate which is going to be your primary language that you continue to use, so long as you understand what the other person is saying? [Yeah.] Okay. "Yeah, I see what you're saying I think about it differently, but that's fine."

Loy
Destination is the same, you have two different routes: you can take that road, I'll get there, and I'm taking this route, same thing. And the function is the same. The functions within the harmonic thing, you can analyze it from C minor, you can analyze it from F, both are valid.

JBJ
So when Shankar is coming in, he's tending to think about things in a much more Carnatic sense or more Hindustani sense?

Loy
His basic thing is Carnatic, he's stronger, but he's also very versatile in Hindustani because he's been exposed to it by now. The only thing is that—it's like me, me telling you "Lydian"

and they call it "Yaman." So the terminology changes, the rest stays the same. There are some rules, like the way you bend the notes, certain rules about that which differs from North and South. Those are cultural things. But talking about modulation, the other song, initially "Kaisi Hai Yeh Rut" the song was in E if I'm not mistaken and Shankar also composed the bridge in E [sings the bridge melody], and I told him "No, move that to G. It will sound better, be modulated and come back to it." So initially, "Is it? Is it?" [Really?] and it was played a couple of times and he said, "Okay, I think." Once you map it to a key, then you have to stay with it, and he's gotten very used to that by now. The first time you're doing it, you're trying it out. We're all teaching each other, and we're all probing. It's the best part of the journey. We learn so much from each other. So then we play that whole G thing, and then put the five (V) chord coming back into the one (I), that was happening. Also, I remember before that we were having a bit of a thing in the studio, an argument about it. I think the song started: I put B opening, a B sus, so in a B pad opening, and the song starts in E. Prior to that there was an F sharp, so it was like a cycle of fourths going on. He was getting very freaked out to sing it, but the people are not going to know what the key of this song is. So I said, "the key of the song is going to be when the melody comes in, they'll hear it." So we were having these slight differences, but it's all part of the creative process.

JBJ
It's interesting to me–probably not as interesting as it is to you–about what songs become popular and why, and sometimes how little control one has over how audiences will receive a song.

Loy
Right. We had no idea it would be such an important album. I think the film also helped very strongly, because if you don't have a film like that, there's no way that you could place these kinds of songs. In some of the older pictures, for example, pull out the song and put this in, it would not work. Really the whole sensibility of the film, kind of be in sync with that because of Farhan. He saw it in a particular way. I think also that there was a void–there was a new India emerging for a lot of the younger people. A little freer, a little more thinking a little beyond the norm. All of the experience, that whole thing of being in college and going on holidays with your buddies. All that kind of fell into place, it locked in, everyone kind of got it.

JBJ
Yeah, and the music captured that too. [Yeah, yeah]. In a lot of the film and cultural criticism that come out of the *Dil Chahta Hai* moment there's this sense that this is the "Millennial soundtrack." [Yes.] If you read YouTube comments or other sorts of commentaries on what *Dil Chahta Hai* did as a film, it was creating this new space, as you were saying, but it also created a new sound. I think that there are a lot of albums and music director approaches that were directly derived from this *Dil Chahta Hai* moment.

Just thinking about where we are today, and the fact that in the classroom I interact mostly with eighteen- to twenty-one-year-olds, I have this strong sense that the listening audience has shifted a little bit in terms of what they expect. They're very comfortable in an entirely electronic space. They don't really feel the need to hear acoustic instruments or regular rock song forms and things along that line. I'm curious, are you seeing that as well on your side?

Loy
Yes, I am also seeing a couple of things that have happened. The shift is also because of two things. You know, when I was growing up, there was basically only radio. I grew up listening to radio. I got a cassette player—I mean, we had a record player, but it was very difficult to get access to a lot of the albums. Then I joined as a member of the USIS [United States Information Service] cultural thing. They had the whole jazz section and the books, and everything, you had access. Then I would tune into Voice of America. I was tuning into "The Now Sound" with Dewey Hughes: all the latest pop songs playing on the radio. It was just a one-hour program. It wasn't FM, it was shortwave—so a lot of disturbance and crap. But we were starved for music, we didn't have access. There were some albums that were very popular, but all the Top 40 stuff was there much later. Bands like The Beatles, they were always available. But that was really popular. If you want something a little more "out of it," some of the other bands took a little while to come in. Yeah, people were traveling and had access to these albums.

As I was saying, today's audience, everyone listens on headphones because everyone's got their own phone. So earlier, what would happen—also India's very family-oriented, right? If there's a TV in the house, everyone watches. It is probably what America used to be in the late '40s, everyone gathered around the radio; that was family time. So that's the same concept out here: there's one television, everyone's watching that. Perhaps if your parents go to bed at night, and you're watching TV alone, that's the only time you can switch to other channels. Otherwise you tend to watch what everyone watches and that's just a little toned down. But today, today, with headphones, you can do your own thing.

7 Interview—Vijay Benegal (Lead Recording and Mixing Engineer)

September 12, 2023, Zoom

Jayson Beaster-Jones
How did you become involved in *Dil Chahta Hai*?

Vijay Benegal
I was really fortunate to get this project because the engineer that they were working with at the time, a colleague of mine– colleague, friend—we were in college at the same time. He was busy on *Mission Kashmir* [SEL's second or third film]. He was in the process of mixing the *Mission Kashmir* album, when this project was starting up. Because he was tied up with that, I got the call up. I am really grateful for that. It was my first full-scale project. I'd been doing a lot of small recordings prior to that— advertising, a couple of small individual songs you know, but just singles, not like a full album or anything. Then this came my way and it sort of established me in the industry because of the nature of the entire project, the film itself. The music, as you know, it kind of introduced a major shift in the business, generally and a lot of people noticed what I had done.

JBJ

So this is kind of a life-changing album for you too, then?

Vijay

Yes, definitely. Okay, I got the IFAA 2002 award for it. It was at the same time as Rahman's *Lagaan*, up against a pretty big gun. And in fact, the guy who was the engineer of *Lagaan*, Sridhar, rest his soul—he passed away some years ago—I learned a few things from him. I did work with him on the surround film mixes for *Dil Chahta Hai* songs. He was a highly respected guy and my work was up against him. Yeah. So it was, it was great.

JBJ

If I understand correctly, you're coming out of heavy metal in the way that you listen—hard rock and heavy metal were your previous projects?

Vijay

Hard rock, yes you could say that was my musical influence. The first album that kind of spun my head, you know, shredded my brain and kind of put it back together, was The Who's *Quadrophenia*. Until that album, I was listening to music, but I was not particularly into anything. This was pretty late in my life, I'd say: I must've been about seventeen or eighteen years old when I first heard this album, and it just blew my mind, literally blew my mind. I was sitting back there when the record finished playing, hearing nothing. "What the hell just hit me?!" So yeah, those British rock bands, Deep Purple, Led Zepplin, The Who, of course. But a big factor in the way I kind of listened to audio. But mostly what influenced my approach to it was Steely Dan, actually.

JBJ

Do you have any memories of what it was like beginning the recording process?

Vijay

Yeah, absolutely. I was lucky enough to be involved from pretty early on almost from the time they started composing. Ehsaan is, incidentally, somebody I've known since we were kids. I mean, I didn't know him very well to begin with. His uncle and my parents knew each other. So we used to meet off and on. But by the time this project had started, we had already become pretty close friends.

JBJ

So you grew up in the same general neighborhoods?

Vijay

Yeah, we were kind of fairly close by, anyway. By the time this project came along, Ehsaan tells me, "Okay, Farhan does not want to sit in Bombay and compose, he wants us to go out of town, to release ourselves from the stresses of the city, and find some peace and quiet and get some inspiration, etc." So I said, "Yeah, that sounds like a plan." And it was a great idea. He says, "but we're going to need some speakers and microphones, can you set us up?" So I figured that out, Ehsaan and me sat in his car, he had a small hatchback. We loaded up the car with a mixer, speakers, a bunch of microphone stands, cables. Just drove it to Khandala—that's about 100 kilometers away from Bombay, on the way to Pune. And we set up in the producer's [Ritesh Sidhwani's] bungalow. And I remember this very clearly: the first thing I did was I had set up the mixer, and I gave Shankar his microphone, and I connected Loy's keyboard. And as I was wiring up the other stuff, Loy comes up with [sings bass line to "Tanhayee"] Shankar starts off [sings "Tanhayee" melody] mouthing words and Javed Akhtar is sitting right there, and he's furiously scribbling. So then, by the time I'm done with getting everybody connected, I think they had maybe 50 percent of the song ready. Things kind of just happened, all really organically. And so the lyrics also being done pretty much alongside. I told Ehsaan, I said, "You know what I'm gonna do (my father lived in this small town around ten or fifteen kilometers further up the road): So I'm gonna go visit him, and I'll come back tomorrow." This was a Saturday. I'd be back Sunday morning. And then I was gonna take a ride back with the producer. So I did that. I came back and they already had another couple of songs ready. They said, "Whoa, this is quick." They had put aside about ten or twelve days for composition, but they were back in a week.

JBJ

So what was the time between when they developed the compositions and when you all started recording?

Vijay

Probably about two weeks, not more than two weeks. Farhan was just ready to go.

JBJ

And where did you record?

Vijay

It was all done here in Bombay at The Fourth Dimension Studios (locally known as 4D)

JBJ

About how long did the recording process itself take?

Vijay

I'd say about thirty or so days: just the recording, and my mixes took me another ten days or so, you know, counting all corrections and changes, and stuff.

JBJ

Did you have to create another mix for the film itself?

Vijay

Oh, yes. But what I did was, I created stereo stems, so like, drums, bass etc, you know. I created a separate set of processed stems, and I took those in. I maintain the essence of the songs and the stereo mix, but kind of spread it out in surround sound for cinema.

JBJ

It sounds like the project as a whole was moving pretty fast.

Vijay

Yeah, that's one of the things that Farhan wanted–once started we went ahead without any breaks—actually, this project changed a lot of things in the industry in general, the scope.

JBJ

Is there anything else that comes to mind thinking of the film itself?

Vijay

We did sync sound in this film, and so another friend and colleague of mine, Nakul Kamte, was the sound designer who took care of all of this. I know that for dialogue, at some point—I don't think he owned it—but at some point he was using the Cedar Systems [platform] to clean up stuff. I don't have too much detail on exactly what he did, but I know for a fact he was talking about Cedar at one point in time. So I think it did happen at least for part of the work.

JBJ
Sync sound gets mentioned in interviews, but I don't think we fully get what kind of an innovation that becomes, unless you've listened to a lot of films. You realize, "Oh, wait, this is why these voices always sound slightly out." The dubbing [ADR, automatic dialogue replacement] makes it sound slightly artificial in terms of the acting.

Vijay
So *Dil Chahta Hai* was—I wouldn't say it's the first film—but it was definitely a major film after a very long time, because early in Indian cinema those did have sync sound. At some point they discovered dubbing is easier, you don't have to worry about dialog so much during the shoot. Farhan decided, "I don't want to go that road. We're doing it." So I think there was about 20 percent of ADR work that was required, kind of industry standard.

JBJ
It does create a different kind of engagement that's on the film. I'm thinking about SEL's recording process. Do you remember how they chose the voices for the particular songs?

Vijay
The lead vocals? Well, it was necessary that Shankar had to sing at least one song, there was no way that Farhan was going to let him go by without singing a song. So obviously he got the title track, and one of the voices in "Koi Kahe." But the other

thing: at that point in time, we didn't have a plethora of good singers, but we did have quite a few well-known singers. Again, there's that little casting that comes in. We want somebody who's a known name, which drove a lot of decisions. Shankar generally chose the singer. If Farhan did not like the idea, essentially Shankar was the one that decided in consultation with Farhan, "Okay, we will use Sonu for this song, we will use Shaan for this song, etc, etc."

JBJ

I've read several interviews where Shankar has said very explicitly that he has spent a lot of time talking film producers out of using his voice for recordings. I can understand why—I just saw him with Shakti [in 2023], and I totally get it. Of course you want to use his voice: the guy's a total badass. Do you remember offhand the other studio musicians you were working with?

Vijay

For bass guitar, that was Karl Peters on two songs: one was "Kaisi Hai Yeh Rut." and "Woh Ladki Hai Kahan"—so two songs were like this. All the other songs, Loy programmed the bass, no loops.

JBJ

I was guessing the drums were probably played by Ranjit [Barot] but I wasn't sure.

Vijay

Actually no, in *Dil Chahta Hai* the acoustic version which is the last song on the album, we recorded on that was live drums, but it wasn't a standard kit. Taufiq Qureshi, who is Zakir

Hussein's youngest brother, he has innovated his own kind of kit, which is a standing kit. The kick drum is not a traditional kick drum, it's like a frame drum. It's tuned low and you get that sound of the kick, but he's playing it by hand with a drum stick.

JBJ
There's this sort of R. D. Burman moment of this pitched percussion that's happening in the Reprise—and that's where it's coming from?

Vijay
Yeah. There's a little bit of trivia on that, particularly that tuned drum. He played the grooves live. We found the best sections, looped them and then layered them with other drum parts, and sections of his live drum were required. (We carried out the same process for "Tanhayee," as well.) That particular tuned drum was a woodblock he was playing. But when he had originally played it, it was starting on the downbeat. As I started mixing the song—or rather, we were still in the process of recording, the guys were taking a break outside to have some tea or something—and I was just cleaning up some stuff, listening to it. Now I said to myself that something is needed, so I just shifted the entire track by an eighth note, so we got that little upbeat. It started bouncing a little bit more. The guys thought this is really good let's keep it.

JBJ
Do you remember what digital audio workstation (DAW) you were using at the time?

Vijay
I used ProTools version 4.3. I remember this so clearly, because I knew nothing of ProTools prior to this recording, except

for maybe an ad in *Mix* magazine or something. I had been recording on analog tape, then on digital tape. Then when we started this recording, we were booked in the studio called 4D, the Fourth Dimension. There were two rooms in that, so Shantanu [Hudlikar] was mixing in the outer room, I was in the other room. The in-house guy says "that's ProTools." So the guys say, "Okay, come on, let's start." I had never seen ProTools in my life! They were getting wired up and you're connecting all the synth stacks and the MIDI connections and all that, so I called, John, the house engineer, I said, "Give me the basics, inputs, outputs, routing, effects, just give me these four things. Then we'll see." By the time he gave me that, we were ready to roll. I mean, Loy said, "Okay, come on, let's start. I've got this program ready. Let's go for it." In fact, I think it was *Dil Chahta Hai*, we started with the title track.

JBJ

Did you use samples for "Woh Ladki"? Did you bring in a fiddle player and a flute player for that?

Vijay

Yeah, there was the fiddle, there was a pipe.

JBJ

It was an Irish tin whistle, or something.

Vijay

Yeah, something like that was programmed as a guide track by Loy, but we layered that with penny whistle and Chinese flute, which Naveen [Kumar] played live. So the initial intent was to get Naveen to do that part. Loy had just programmed it as a reference. After we recorded Naveen, Shankar said, "let's just hear the whole stack (live plus programmed parts). Let's see what it sounds like." It kind of sounded nicer. So, yeah, let's just keep it that way.

JBJ
Most of the time that I've heard Naveen play, it's been in an Indian classical style. So I've been assuming that he's been primarily playing *bansuri*, but does he play Western flute as well?

Vijay
Man, he's got an armory! But he did come in with a couple of cases full of different kinds of flutes. As far as I know he's got a shakuhachi somewhere in his arsenal as well. I mean, he's got a lot.

JBJ
So for "Kaisi Hai Yeh Rut" he would have been playing all the flutes there overdubbed?

Vijay
Absolutely, same with "Tanhayee." This was a completely overdubbed album and there were no simultaneous recording of musicians. There was programmed stuff, everything was dubbed on top of that. Taufiq was playing his drums: what we did was, we recorded some parts individually, some things, such as his standing kit, and we'd find the best four bars or eight bars and loop those, take different sections for different parts. In fact, that "Tanhayee" groove we pretty much did it for the whole song, and then I fiddled with it. In some sections, I would mute out some stuff and bring it in the next section. So I did a little bit of an edit myself. Then Shankar came in, says, "I like this, let's keep half of this and we'll change it this way." So the edit also was like a very collaborative effort.

JBJ

In "Tanhayee," it sounds like Loy used an analog synth for the bass, but I know that he used a digital synth to get that sound.

Vijay

We didn't have any analog synths, unfortunately. But he did use some samples of some Moog. We are going to just highlight that particular [sound] because of my own personal background with analog. When we started recording this, I was like "No. This is digital, but quite different from ADAT," but it was not exciting me as much as I thought it should. I was still very much thinking in analog terms. The way the studio was laid out, the console was closer to the front, Loy was sitting behind me in the far corner. So, he was actually in a very bad place to be sitting because of a lot of bass build up over there, and he did a lot of programming in the studio. I had to sit there and help him with some of the choices of the sounds of whatever instruments he was using from his synths from his MIDI setup. I would say, "you know, Loy, I think we've got too much of this, drop that, increase this," etc. So we kind of worked together on the sound a lot. I suppose that's why maybe some of the synths are a little analog-ish. I also tracked them, some of them. I can't remember which ones, but there were a couple of them, which I ran through an analog compressor and there were just two compressors there: put it through that just to add some different textures into it.

JBJ

I appreciate the analog sounds where they are. "Tanhayee" is a great example of that phat kind of Moog kind of sound that works really well. But it's interesting to think about the production process and how much is happening in the studio over many days, and how and how projects evolve. With regard to this, you said that you multitracked everything. This includes the background vocals as well?

Vijay
So, regarding the background vocals, I actually was just going through the sessions, and I was just trying to figure out what I had done. We did it in two different ways. It varied from song to song and there was no specific reason for doing it one way or the other, it's just what I just felt like at that point in time. So one way of doing it was we had a single microphone, Neumann U87, and I set it up in cardioid [pattern]. And I had my four background vocalists around. They were four: two males, two females. Clinton Cerejo was the leader, there was Dominique [now Cerejo], there was Kunal [Ganjawala] and Gayatri [Iyer]. Caralisa [Monteiro] did a solo part in "Jaane Kyon." Clinton was mainly the guy that arranged the vocals and stuff. We would record, say, all four of them singing one part, then double track that, would pan that left, right, then we would do that with the next voice in the harmony. So that was one way we did it. Another way we did it was I did an XY pair, but I think I only did that for one track. I'm not certain which one, but I think I only used it once. What we did was in some harmonies, Clinton wrote the different voicing, so all four of them were singing on that one take, then double that on another take. A couple of unison tracks, then one track which has got two or three voices. Another track which has got two three voices kind of blended for that. These four guys as a group were really good. Your comment about them being very tight is because they rehearsed those parts on the spot. They're really good.

JBJ
Regarding the didgeridoo in "Jaane Kyon," did you bring someone in for that?

Vijay

I wish we could have but we didn't. However, Nakul [Kamte] happened to be shooting in Australia, so he got it done. It is a live didgeridoo but it was recorded in Australia and they just sent us the file.

JBJ

For that song I know that the background vocalists are using some vocables with some nonsense words and things along that line. Is it the same group of four people who are singing that?

Vijay

Yeah. So there are two solo vocals, Caralisa and Clinton. At the end they do it as a chorus, in the middle bridge section there's the solo. That's the idea. Yeah, that's nonsense syllables. At the end there's the "ookuoo misa looway loowah" nonsense lyrics in chorus.

JBJ

Did you have a favorite track in this project?

Vijay

My favorite track would probably be the "Dil Chahta Hai (Reprise)," mainly because of the effort that I had to put in: that was a purely acoustic track. And "Tanhayee," as well because there was a lot of acoustical recording work that I had to do. But in terms of just songs, I liked, let's just say "Dil Chahta Hai," "Tanhayee," the Reprise, for sure. Then after that would be "Woh Ladki Hai Kahan." "Jaane Kyon" was the first hit song, actually, of the album. And I didn't like it. But I started liking it a bit later, but just didn't like it at the time.

JBJ

Are there any other things that come to mind with this soundtrack and its broader influence that you might talk about?

Vijay

I just discovered that this colleague of mine, P, who I was working with earlier today, about how he got to know about me. Another engineer, C, who I've worked with in the past, said to him, "Listen, you have to listen to this album, *Dil Chahta Hai*." And P said, "I've heard it." C says "No, no, no, really listen to it." Then he was telling me that, his words, is that as he and listened to it, and was totally amazed at the overall, recording, mixing, production, and compositions. So definitely, whatever it was, the sound of the album made people sit up and listen. I'm talking about engineers and musicians as well, because this was a very fresh new approach. So, it's not just not only my thing, a lot of contribution from—I mean, primarily it's the music itself that made people sit up and listen a lot. It influenced the industry in a huge way. And people started working differently, just composing differently, recording differently. But I think you're talking about the length or the longevity of the influence. I think it's kind of died down because people are producing crap nowadays. It's just awful shit. I mean, I'm sorry, for the language, but I can't find a more polite way of describing it.

JBJ

All of this bedroom pop, bedroom hip hop, and things like that people are able to produce on their own seems to appeal to a Gen Z ear in a way that it probably doesn't appeal to earlier generations.

Vijay

Yeah. And I think it's also got to do with the way consumption of music, how music is being consumed. Everything is short term, it is not like when you had to go out and buy a vinyl record, and you took so much care of that record, and you would place it, you'd sit down and listen, you would get up, turn it over again. Listen, you know, you got involved with the music.

JBJ

What you're saying is that audiences are not listening closely enough?

Vijay

Yeah. I remember in my day I got obsessed with the Who, blew my mind. So Shantanu and me, we were in college together and we used to lock ourselves into a room and pull records out and play them over and over. We were listening in depth, reading all the liner notes. Where was this recorded? Who's the recording engineer? I mean, this was way before we even realized that there is such a job as a recording engineer. Without realizing it we were listening the way engineers and producers would listen to music. I can tell you that one of the big producers of the day at that point was Martin Birch. He did like a lot of Deep Purple and Rainbow, Black Sabbath, and others. This is stuff I remember from them. Not because I know it today. We spent so much time on reading the credits. These days people don't even know who's singing.

JBJ

So the point that you make about the influence of *Dil Chahta Hai* having waned, it sounds like it's not just this album, but a particular style of soundtrack making, or a particular style of song production that's moved in a different direction.

Vijay
I think, you know … Okay, this is my analysis of it—I couldn't put any concrete evidence towards this conclusion—but what's happened is that in the Hindi film business, probably the film business all over the country, budgets are dictating who is going to get the project. So it's very, very few big budget, rather biggish budget projects that go to a big name like an SEL, or a Vishal-Shekhar or somebody like that. In the larger scheme of things, it's because the budgets are so low. I mean, production is just squeezing everyone all around. So the composer is the guy who asks for the least amount of money which means you're probably going to get a much more mediocre composition.

JBJ
My hypothesis, and I'd be curious to see what you would think of this, is that *Dil Chahta Hai* in particular created a space in the early 2000s–2010s for your Vishal-Shekhars or for your Salim-Sulaimans, your Amit Trivedis. You know that in essence, once you could see what was possible with *Dil Chahta Hai* and then other music directors start seeing more work as a result of that.

Vijay
Yes definitely, because some of them were coming from a similar background musically. So the Vishal-Shekhar: Vishal [Dadlani] was a rocker, electronica, and metal. And Shekhar [Ravjiani] is coming from more of a [Indian] classical background. So that combination, I think people kind of figured that, "Okay, we can do this: we blend Western and Indian, because this is a

great success story, right?" Just to add to that, with SEL, they had three influences: jazz, blues and rock, and [Indian] classical. That was rather wide, so it worked really well.

JBJ
Is there anything else that I should be asking you that I'm not?

Vijay
My process during the recording for *Dil Chahta Hai*. This is how the day would start, I live relatively close to Ehsaan, I would take a little autorickshaw from my place to his house and we would pile into that little hatchback of his. In the car, we would crank up the stereo, blasting Van Halen or Led Zepplin depending on whatever we wanted all the way to the studio. So now we've blasted our ears out we get down to recording. We spent the whole day recording. End of the day, whatever time it was, eight o'clock, nine o'clock, depending on what changed from day to day, I would tell Ehsaan, "Okay, you head out. I'm staying back." I would stay back for an hour, sometimes two hours depending on what was required. If there was a lot of cleaning up and editing work to be done, then I would rebalance the tracks for the next day so that when we come in the morning, we'd know what we've done, and then we can move forward from that. That was my process. By the time we came to the mixing stage, songs were pretty much mixed. I was giving myself the time to EQ something, put in some effect experiment with a delay or some processing. "Okay, Shankar, do you like this on the voice?" "Yeah I like this." We keep it, you know, that kind of thing. By the time we got there, we were very close to a mix. And as it turns out, with the title track, at the end when we finally said, "Okay, now that's it. We're done. No more recording." The mix that finally went on to the album was a so-called "rough mix." It

wasn't the final final mix (which I had done). But yeah, that's the one that everybody, myself included, said like, no, actually, this has got a much better vibe than the final mix.

8 Interview—Michael Harvey (Composer)

July 5, 2023, Zoom

Jayson Beaster-Jones
How did you get involved in the *Dil Chahta Hai* project?

Michael Harvey
There was an associate in Australia, John Senczuk, who I had worked with on two other productions, one at the Sydney Theatre Company, and another, a musical called *Lush*, which was about the singer that I worked with. So it was through John—and he put me in touch with Ritesh Sidhwani [DCH producer]. I met with him and, and a lot of the direction then came through Ritesh to John and then to me. But it was a pretty blank canvas to be honest. They said, "we're going to the opera. It's going to be held in the State Theater, we want you to write several short excerpts that could be from an opera. You don't have to write the whole opera." So I wrote six segments—arias and themes.

JBJ
These were six mini compositions a minute or two each?

Michael
Yes, that's right. There was the overture which was 2 minutes and twenty seconds, the aria, which was really a minute and a half, the ballet which is 2 minutes, the tenor aria, the marketplace scene, which was a minute, and the duet. After I completed my recordings, they must have decided to edit two or three of them together. I'm not sure what happened in the film process because I wasn't ever in the theater. After the recording and staging I met again with Ritesh, he said he was happy with the result. Then they went into post-production to mix and edit.. And I believe at that point, they made some changes to the script, and to the film.

JBJ
So you provided them with the written compositions, but you weren't involved with the recording?

Michael
Oh yes, I conducted and produced the recording. I wrote the orchestrations. We recorded at Studios 301 in Sydney, which at the time was probably the biggest and best studio in Sydney. We engaged the orchestra and singers and recorded it all at 301.

JBJ
My hypothesis has been that the overture that you wrote became what they called "Aakash's Theme." Is that correct?

Michael
Yes, that's correct Jayson.

JBJ

How long did it take you to compose it and to get the final approval from Ritesh [Sidhwani]?

Michael

Well, I wrote the composition over a couple of days. I did a sketch first of the compositions, just on piano, and that was approved. So I went into the studio, over two days (about five hours each day), then back in to mix the next day. It wasn't a long period of time, because it was originally only about twelve minutes of music. Then it was played to Ritesh, he enjoyed it. He liked it a lot—I think he said something like, "Yes, that sounds great." I believe they had some staging difficulties at the State Theater and that might have brought about the changes—that is, not showing the whole sequence of the opera, I'm not sure.

JBJ

I would have been surprised if the whole scene had lasted twelve minutes, because I suspect that they may not have been able to keep the attention of the audience and the narrative flow of the film. I know that they brought the theme back a couple of more times in the film score. Just as an aside, that it's fairly uncommon for music directors to have a theme that they associate with a particular character. The fact that they included this composition in the soundtrack is just fascinating to me because it almost never happens.

Michael

I was thrilled when they did. I think that one of the reviews said something about the *Gone with the Wind* moment, referred to it that way. I was quite chuffed, actually.

JBJ

What language was the libretto of the piece you composed?

Michael

It was in French. There was a Massenet opera that had been mentioned to me. I didn't listen to it too closely—as a composer you want to keep a clear head, to stay original. But I was definitely listening to operas with similar plots, to put me into the frame of mind to compose the piece. Then, I got away from everything for a few days before I started writing.

JBJ

When did you first hear the final recording as it was used in the film?

Michael

Many years later, in fact, not until it was released on DVD.

JBJ

Did you feel like there was a match between how you envisioned it was going to be seen onscreen and the music that you wrote?

Michael

It was a little different because I thought that they would include the music in specific parts of the film: they'd come back to the opera and see the specific parts of the opera that related to the drama … When you see this movie, and you hear the juxtaposition of the opera against the contemporary music score, you do think "it's good that it's different," When I watched the film the first time I thought, "Oh, this actually works better than I thought it was going to be" because I had not heard the rest of the soundtrack first. And I then thought they're two completely different genres—it does work.

JBJ
The choice of *Troilus and Cressida*, was that your choice or was that their choice?

Michael
Troilus and Cressida was suggested to me, but I'm not sure who it came from.

JBJ
There are some Shakespearean literary critics who've made a case that *Dil Chahta Hai* is based very loosely on *Much Ado About Nothing*. They're citing the use of *Troilus and Cressida*, which of course is a Shakespeare play, as part of the argument that they're making. I don't know whether you know whether that idea has any legitimacy or not: the film director, Farhan Akhtar, has denied actually knowing anything about *Much Ado*, and he has said that never seen it or read it which is probably fair. Yet it strikes me that if you put a template up to any story, it's going to be Shakespearean at some point.

Michael
Hmm, yes I see—there was no mention at all about *Much Ado*, but *Troilus and Cressida* was mentioned, and the fact that they were going to stage something like that. I didn't source any particular material at the time but I listened to Massenet and Puccini, who I love—I just listened to a selection of operatic music and got myself into the head space, as I often do.

Personnel

Shankar Mahadevan—Co-composer, singer ("Dil Chahta Hai," "Koi Kahe," "Dil Chahta Hai—Reprise")

Ehsaan Noorani—Co-composer, guitars, synths

Loy Mendonsa—Co-composer, keyboards, synths

Michael Harvey—Composer ("Akash's Love Theme")

Javed Akhtar—Lyrics

Udit Narayan—Singer ("Jaane Kyon")

Alka Yagnik—Singer ("Jaane Kyon")

Shaan—Singer ("Woh Ladki," "Koi Kahe")

Kavita Krishnamurthy—Singer ("Woh Ladki")

Srinivas—Singer ("Kaisi Hai")

KK—Singer ("Koi Kahe")

Sonu Nigam—Singer ("Tanhayee")

Clinton Cerejo—Vocal Arranger, Background Vocals

Dominique Cerejo—Background Vocals

Gayatri Iyer—Background Vocals

Kunal Ganjawala- Background Vocals

Caralisa Monteiro—Background Vocals (guest solo in "Jaane Kyon")

Karl Peters—Bass ("Kaisi Hai," "Yeh Ladki")

Taufiq Quresh—Drums ("Tanhayee," "Kaisi Hai," "Dil Chahta Hai (Reprise)")

Naveen Kumar—Flutes ("Woh Ladki," "Kaisi Hai," "Tanhayee")

Vijay Benegal—Recording and Mixing Engineer

Recorded in Fourth Dimension Studios in Mumbai.

Works Cited

Adarsh, Taran. 2002. "Dil Chahta Hai Movie Review." https://www.bollywoodhungama.com/movie/dil-chahta-hai/critic-review/dil-chahta-hai-movie-review/; Accessed 2/4/2024.

Akhtar, Farhan. 2001. "The Making of Dil Chahta Hai, Part IV." https://www.youtube.com/watch?v=al28vM8VCKI; Accessed 2/5/2024.

Akhtar, Javed and Nasreen Munni Kabir. 2005. *Talking Songs: Javed Akhtar in Conversation with Nasreen Munni Kabir and Sixty Selected Songs*. Delhi: Oxford University Press.

Appadurai, Arjun. 1996. *Modernity at Large: Cultural Dimensions of Globalization*. Minneapolis: University of Minnesota Press.

Balial, Nandini. 2022. "How Dil Chahta Hai Raised the Bar for Commercial Hindi Cinema." https://www.rogerebert.com/features/dil-chahta-hai-feature-2022; Accessed 2/5/2024.

Beaster-Jones, Jayson. 2009. "Evergreens to Remixes: Hindi Film Songs and India's Popular Music Heritage." *Ethnomusicology* 53(3): 425–48.

Beaster-Jones, Jayson. 2015. *Bollywood Sounds: The Cosmopolitan Mediations of Hindi Film Song*. New York: Oxford University Press.

Beaster-Jones, Jayson. 2017. "A.R. Rahman and the Aesthetic Transformation of Indian Film Scores." *Special Issue: The Evolution of Song and Dance in Hindi Cinema*, Edited by Ajay Gehlawat and Rajinder Dudrah. *South Asian Popular Culture* 15(2–3): 155–71.

Booth, Gregory. 2008. *Behind the Curtain: Making Music in Mumbai's Film Studios*. New York: Oxford University Press.

Chattopadhyay, Budhaditya. 2021. *Between the Headphones: Listening to the Practitioner*. Newcastle: Cambridge Scholars Press.

Coventry, Chloe. 2013. *Rock Bands/Rock Brands: Mediation and Musical Performance in Post-liberalization Bangalore*. Unpublished Ph.D. Dissertation, University of California, Los Angeles.

Filmanter. 2022. "Dil Chahta Hai—Making of a 'Timeless' Movie." https://www.youtube.com/watch?v=bPQ3T7TTroI; Accessed 2/5/2024.

Ganti, Tejaswini. 2012. *Producing Bollywood: Inside the Contemporary Hindi Film Industry*. Durham: Duke University Press.

Ganti, Tejaswini. 2013. *Bollywood: A Guidebook to Popular Hindi Cinema, 2nd Edition*. New York: Routledge.

Gehlawat, Ajay. 2017. "The Picture Is Not Yet Over!: The End Credits Song Sequence in Bollywood." *South Asian Popular Culture* 15(2–3): 203–16.

Getter, Joseph and B. Balasubrahmaniyan. 2008. "Tamil Film Music: Sound and Significance" in *Global Soundtracks: Worlds of Film Music*, Mark Slobin, ed. Middletown, CT: Wesleyan University Press, 114–51.

Goodwin, Andrew. 1992. *Dancing in the Distraction Factory: Music Television and Popular Culture*. Minneapolis: University of Minnesota Press.

IANS. 2010. "'Dil Chahta Hai' Saved Goa Tourism Post 9/11 Gloom." https://www.deccanherald.com/content/105091/dil-chahta-hai-saved-goa.html; Accessed 2/5/2024.

IANS. 2020. "Farah Khan Explains Famous 'Dil Chahta Hai' Dance Step." https://gulfnews.com/entertainment/bollywood/farah-khan-explains-famous-dil-chahta-hai-dance-step-1.74630115#; Accessed 2/5/2024.

Kvetko, Peter. 2005. *Indipop: Producing Global Sounds and Local Meanings in Bombay (India)*. Unpublished Ph.D. Dissertation, University of Texas.

Kvetko, Peter. 2009. "Private Music: Individualism, Authenticity and Genre Boundaries in the Bombay Music Industry" in *Popular Culture in a Globalised India*, K. Moti Gokulsing and Wimal Dissanayake, eds. New York: Routledge, 111–24.

Lukose, Ritty. 2009. *Liberalization's Children: Gender, Youth, and Consumer Citizenship in Globalizing India*. Durham, NC: Duke University Press.

Manuel, Peter. 1993. *Cassette, Culture: Popular Music and Industry in North India*. Chicago: University of Chicago Press.

Morcom, Anna. 2007. *Hindi Film Songs and the Cinema*. Burlington, VT: Ashgate.

Pathak, Ankur. 2021. "Friends." https://fiftytwo.in/story/friends/; Accessed 2/5/2024.

Pillai, Meena T. 2012. "Post-national B(H)ollywood and the National Imaginary" in *The Magic Of Bollywood: At Home and Abroad*, Anjali Gera Roy, ed. New Delhi: Sage, 48–54.

Rizvi, Zafar. 2021. "19 Years of Dil Chahta Hai—A Film That Rewrote the Rules of the Game." https://www.highonfilms.com/dil-chahta-hai-a-film-that-rewrote-the-rules-of-the-game; Accessed 2/5/2024.

Sarrazin, Natalie. 2008. "Celluloid Love Songs: Musical Modus Operandi and the Dramatic Aesthetics of Romantic Hindi Film." *Popular Music* 27: 393–411.

Sarrazin, Natalie. Forthcoming. "The Beatles, the Bands and Bollywood: Dialectical Identities of India's Popular Music." *South Asian History and Culture*.

Valika-Gilani, Alavia. 2021. "Celebrating 20 Years of the Cult Classic *Dil Chahta Hai*." https://www.filmcompanion.in/readers-articles/dil-chahta-hai-hindi-movie-celebrating-20-years-of-the-cult-classic-aamir-khan-saif-ali-khan-akshaye-khan-farhan-akhtar; Alavia Valika-Gilani; August 6, 2021; Accessed 2/5/2024.

Vats, Vatsala Devki. 2020. "19 Years on, Dil Chahta Hai Continues to Remain a Masterpiece Film on Friendship." https://www.indiatimes.com/entertainment/bollywood/19-years-on-dil-chahta-hai-continues-to-remain-a-masterpiece-film-on-friendship-518289.html; Accessed 2/5/2024.

Verma, Sukanya. 2001. "Dil Chahta Hai Music Review." https://m.rediff.com/movies/2001/jun/25dil.htm; Accessed 2/5/2024.

Weinstein, Deena. 2000. *Heavy Metal: A Cultural Sociology*. Boston: Da Capo Press.

Discography

The Beach Motion Picture Soundtrack (Sire Records, 2000).
Bollywood Flashback (Columbia, 1994).

Filmography

Bhaag Milkha Bhaag. 2013. Director: Rakeysh Omprakash Mehra. Music: Shankar-Ehsaan-Loy. Rakeysh Omprakash Mehra Pictures, Mumbai.

Bombay. 1995. Director: Mani Ratnam. Music: A. R. Rahman. Amitabh Bachchan Corporation Limited, Mumbai.

Bunty Aur Babli. 2005. Director: Shaad Ali. Music: Shankar-Ehsaan-Loy. Yash Raj Films, Mumbai.

Dil Chahta Hai. 2001. Director: Fahran Akhtar. Music: Shankar-Ehsaan-Loy. Excel Entertainment, Mumbai.

Dilwale Dulhania Le Jayenge. 1995. Director: Aditya Chopra. Music: Jatin-Lalit. Yashraj Films, Mumbai.

Don. 2006. Director: Farhan Akhtar. Music: Shankar-Ehsaan-Loy. Excel Entertainment, Mumbai.

Kabhi Khushi Kabhie Gham. 2001. Director: Karan Johar. Music: Jatin-Lalit. Dharma Productions, Mumbai.

Kal Ho Na Ho. 2003. Director: Nikhil Advani. Music: Shankar-Ehsaan-Loy. Dharma Productions, Mumbai.

Lagaan. 2001. Director: Ashutosh Gowariker. Music: A. R. Rahman. Aamir Khan Productions, Mumbai.

The Last Temptation of Christ. 1988. Director: Martin Scorsese. Universal Pictures, Hollywood.

Mission Kashmir. 2000. Director: Vidhu Vinod Chopra. Music: Shankar-Eshaan-Loy. Vinod Chopra Productions, Mumbai.

My Name Is Khan. 2010. Director: Karan Johar. Music: Shankar-Ehsaan-Loy. Dharma Productions, Mumbai.

Rock On!! 2008. Director: Abhishek Kapoor. Music: Shankar-Ehsaan-Loy. Excel Entertainment, Mumbai.

Roja. 1993. Director: Mani Rathnam. Music: A. R. Rahman. Hansa Pictures, Chennai.

Slumdog Millionaire. 2008. Director: Danny Boyle. Music: A. R. Rahman. Searchlight Pictures, Hollywood.

Swades. 2004. Director: Ashutosh Gowariker. Music: A. R. Rahman. Ashutosh Gowariker Productions, Mumbai.

Zindagi Na Milegi Dobara. 2011. Director: Zoya Akhtar. Music: Shankar-Ehsaan-Loy. Excel Entertainment, Mumbai.

Index

advertising films 5, 7, 16, 29, 65, 71, 78, 81, 95
Afro Celt Sound System 58–9, 71
Akash (character) 9–11, 34–5, 40, 42, 44–5
"Akash's love theme" 11, 42–3, 113–14
Akhtar, Farhan xx, 15, 31, 38, 40, 55, 57, 61, 72, 97–100, 117
Akhtar, Javed 25, 26, 32, 36, 38, 41, 45, 52, 63, 86–7, 98
Akhtar, Zoya 63
Anand, Mukul 29, 68
audiences xiv, 7, 13–14, 16, 34, 43, 80–1, 91–3, 108–9, 115
Australia xiii, 34, 42–3, 44, 61, 107, 113
awards 51

background score 43, 82, 116
backing vocals 20, 23, 32, 39, 106
Benegal, Vijay xx, 27, 52, 58, 63, Chapter 7
Bhaag Milkha Bhaag 37
Bhosle, Asha 6, 24
Birch, Martin 109
Bombay 16
bridge, musical 25, 31, 64, 107
Burman, R.D. xvi, xvii, 16, 25, 42, 102

cassettes 7–8, 93
Cerejo, Clinton xx, 106
Chapora Fort 30–1, 47
choir 20, 21, 23, 32
choreography 13, 36
classical, Indian 6, 27, 35, 44, 70, 77, 85, 90–1
classical, Western 43, 77
clave xii, 41
colonialism 3–4
composition retreat 37, 57–8, 97–8
compositional process 26, 60–3, 75, 78–9, 104–5, 111–2
consumerism 3–4

dance hook 36
Dance Masti 8
didgeridoo xii, 34, 61, 106–7
digital audio workstations (DAW) xvi, 19, 23, 26, 102
Dil Chahta Hai film 9–11, 49–51, 92, 110, 117
"Dil Chahta Hai (Reprise)" 11, 46–7, 66, 102, 107
"Dil Chahta Hai" (title song) 9, 30–3, 46–7, 59–60, 64–5, 87–8, 103
Dil Se 16, 46
disco 41, 42
Don 70, 71

drone 21, 44–5, 84
Dus 29, 57, 68

electronic dance music (EDM) 41–2, 61, 71
ensemble (orchestration) 20, 22–3, 114

film song xv, 7, 11–15, 55, 68
film song conventions 14–15, 52, 87
film song in narrative 15–16
film song production 12–13
Filmfare 36, 51
flute (bansuri) 38–9, 44–5, 103–4
folk music 6, 27, 34

Ganjawala, Kunal 106
ghazal 6–7, 38
globalization xi–xii
Goa 9, 11, 30–1
guitar 20, 24–5, 32–3, 37, 61, 64–5, 72, 88

harmony 6, 20, 21–2, 33, 35, 37–9, 74, 78–9, 82–5, 89
Harvey, Michael 42, Chapter 8
Hudlikar, Shantanu 103, 109

Indipop xvii, 5–6, 8, 14, 24
influences, musical 20, 42, 51, 52, 61, 71, 75, 77–9, 84
Instant Karma 42, 52

"Jaane Kyon" xii, xiii, 10, 23, 33–5, 51, 52, 59, 61, 74, 79, 106, 107
Jatin-Lalit 16, 23, 32

jazz 22, 38, 39, 47, 66, 71, 77, 80–1, 87, 93
jingles 7, 29, 65, 69, 78, 81

Kabhi Khushi Kabhie Gham xvi, 23, 32, 51
"Kaisi Hai Yeh Rut" 10, 22, 37–9, 73, 91, 101, 104
Kal Ho Na Ho xvi, 45, 58, 70
Kamte, Nakul 99–100, 107
Kapadia, Dimple 9
Khan, Aamir 9, 34
Khan, Farah 36, 40
Khan, Saif Ali 9, 44
Khanna, Akshaye 9
KK 6, 40
"Koi Kahe" 10, 39–42, 52, 61, 89, 100
Krishnamurthy, Kavita xii, 24, 36–7
Kulkarni, Sonali 9
Kumar, Kishore 6, 24, 46
Kumar, Naveen 38, 46, 103–4

Lagaan xvi, 50, 51, 96
Lahiri, Bappi xvii, 42
Laxmikant-Pyarelal xvi, 16, 23, 30, 32
liberalization 3–4, 41, 50
lip sync 31, 37–8, 44, 99–100
live performance 67
lyricist 12–14, 51
lyrics xviii, 31–2, 36–7, 43–4, 47, 51, 116

Mahadevan, Shankar xx, 29, 31, 40, 47, 55, 59, 68–70, 77, 86–9, 97–8, 100–1, 103–4

Malik, Anu xvii, 16
Mangeshkar, Lata 6, 24
mediation xiii–xiv, 15, 26, 33, 110–1
melody 13, 25, 45, 62, 78–9, 84
Mendonsa, Loy xx, 29, 35, 42, 45, 47, 52, 55, 68–70, 73, Chapter 6, 97–8, 103, 105
military music 79–80
millennial soundtrack 21, 41, 50–1, 92
Mission Kashmir 49, 79, 95
modulation, harmonic 37, 39, 89, 91
Monteiro, Caralisa 106
mukhda-antara form xiv, 25, 29, 32, 33, 40, 63–4, 74
music director 12–15, 21
music television 5–6, 16

Narayan, Udit xiii, 6, 34–5, 51–2
Nigam, Sonu 6, 44–6
Noorani, Ehsaan xx, 24–5, 29, 32, 42, 52, 55, Chapter 5, 77, 88, 97–8

opera 11, 42–3, 113–14, 116
orchestral score 12

Peters, Karl 22, 101
picturization xii, 13–14, 37–8, 40
playback singers 6, 16, 24, 100–1
Pooja (character) 9–10, 36–7
ProTools 60, 73, 102–3

Qureshi, Taufiq 22, 101–2, 104

Raamlaxman 16
radio 12, 16, 68, 86, 93
Rafi, Mohammed 6, 24, 46
raga 46, 85–7, 90–1
Rahman, A.R. xiii, xvi, 7, 15, 20, 23, 24, 44, 46, 61, 96
recording studio 19–20, 23, 26, 59–60
remix 8, 42
riffs x, xii, 20–21, 36–7, 67, 75, 78
rock band aesthetic xiii, xvi, 17, 20, 26, 29–30, 33, 37, 39, 46, 52
Rock On 61–2, 70, 75
"Rockin' Goa" 9, 71–2
Roja 16, 46

Sagoo, Bally 8, 42
Salim-Sulaiman 110
Sameer (character) 9–10, 36–7, 40
Shaan xii, 36–7, 40
Shalini (character) 9–11, 34–5, 40, 42, 44
Shankar-Ehsaan-Loy (SEL) 15, 19–20, 45–6, 78
Shankar-Jaikishan xvi
Sid (character) 9–10, 37–8, 40
Sidhwani, Ritesh 15, 42, 57, 97, 113, 115
Singh, Sukhwinder 6
song form 25, 33, 39, 63–4
song situation 12–14, 59, 62
sound (aesthetic) 20, 26–7, 52, 69–70, 105, 108
sound engineer 13, 27
Srinivas 38

string orchestra 20, 22–3, 33, 39
synchronized sound 50–1
synthesizer 21, 71, 88–9, 105

Taal 16, 46
"Tanhayee" 11, 22, 35, 44–6, 86–7, 89, 102, 104, 107
Tara (character) 9–10, 37–8
techno 41–2 (*see also* EDM)
television 5–6, 12, 81
trance 61, 71 (*see also* EDM)
translation xviii
Trivedi, Amit xvi, 110
Troilus and Cressida 11, 117

verse-chorus form xiv, 33
Vishal-Shekhar 110–1
Voice of America 93

Western music xi, 6–7, 16, 20, 21, 23, 25, 32, 39, 47, 64, 68, 82–3, 90, 96
"Woh Ladki Hai Kahan" xii, 10, 35–7, 52, 59, 79, 101, 107
world music 61, 79

Yagnik, Alka xiii, 6, 24, 34–5, 52
youth x–xi, 4, 16, 50, 52, 78, 93

Zindagi Na Milegi Dobara xvi, 70
Zinta, Priety 9

www.ingramcontent.com/pod-product-compliance
Lightning Source LLC
Chambersburg PA
CBHW070555160426
43199CB00014B/2511